A REAL ESTATE AGENT'S GUIDE TO SUCCESSFUL SALES AND LISTINGS

A REAL ESTATE AGENT'S GUIDE TO SUCCESSFUL SALES AND LISTINGS

Charlotte Korn

RESTON PUBLISHING COMPANY, INC.
Reston, Virginia
A Prentice-Hall Company

Library of Congress Cataloging in Publication Data

Korn, Charlotte.
    A real estate agent's guide to successful sales and
listings.

    Includes index.
    1. Real estate business.   I. Title.
HD1375.K6   333.3'3   76-17028
ISBN 0-87909-711-6

© 1976 by
Reston Publishing Company, Inc.
A Prentice-Hall Company
Reston, Virginia 22090

10   9   8   7   6   5   4   3

Printed in the United States of America.

To my sons, STAN, BOB and ED

and especially to my husband, ALEX, whose encouragement, patience and understanding contributed to my sales career and to this book.

CONTENTS

PREFACE

Real estate salesmanship is one field where maturity can be a plus. It is never too late to become a salesman! I had just had my fiftieth birthday, when my husband told me about a real estate course being given downtown. I remembered an ad in the local papers, in which a real estate company offered free instructions. With no previous experience in direct selling, I enrolled in the class, bought the required book on real estate, and found a new, stimulating and exciting way of life. I read the book continually until I had almost memorized it. I then took the real estate test, passed the test, and a new world of recognition and rewards opened for me.

In my second year of real estate selling, I was the "Top Agent in the County" and in my third year I was "Top Lister in the County." Not only did my commissions mount up, but I received many awards, trophies, and bonuses—including a Cadillac, a color television set and cruises. The local newspapers wrote glowing articles and carried my picture. I expected all the local homeowners to immediately beat a path to my real estate door, begging me to list their homes, and/or to find other homes for them. There actually was a surge of phone calls.

However, they were not from anxious sellers of homes, but rather from anxious agents working in other real estate offices, inquiring as follows:

Hello, is this Charlotte? You probably don't know me. Our sales manager talks about you constantly. He told us that you were making lots of money listing and selling homes, and that you were very cooperative. I am quite new in real estate and have not been doing too well. As a matter of fact, I am waiting for my baby sitter now, and have fifteen minutes to spare before she gets here. *Can you tell me all you know?*

This is now my tenth year in real estate and I have been continually asked by other agents and friends, "How do you do it? You seem to be having fun and it looks so easy. Yet, you are making all that money, too."

In this book, I describe my successful techniques. Many are original. Some have been inherited from others and then developed and tailored to my personal needs. All have been working for me. There is every reason to expect them to work for other agents, who, like myself, have decided that real estate selling is a most interesting career.

The two most important sections of any practical book on real estate agents must be **listing** and **selling** (Chapters Two and Five in this book). If you are an experienced agent, you may wish to start directly with Chapter Two "Good Listings are like Having Money in the Bank." Chapter One "If Real Estate is Your Thing" is principally for the new agent or anyone thinking about becoming a real estate agent. Knowledge of financing which has become most important for the salesman in recent years is covered in Chapter Four. A separate chapter (Chapter Six) is devoted to "After You Have The Contract Offer" as I have found many agents are not trained in the best way to make a presentation of an offer. Chapter Seven "You Are In Business For Yourself" is not a topic normally found in books on real estate, but of great interest to agents. The Glossary is a ready reference to the "trade" terminology I use in the book (which may differ in other areas of the country) and also includes terms with which the new agent might not be familiar.

The highest paid salesmen in the world follow a program of self-improvement by keeping up with the latest publications in their field and attending clinics and seminars. Selling techniques change with the times. New methods of dealing with people are continually advanced. Success in selling real estate usually comes as a result of hard work, experience and knowledge of what works best. This book will contribute to that knowledge and help you become successful and prosperous.

CHARLOTTE KORN

chapter one

IF REAL ESTATE
IS YOUR THING

▪ GETTING STARTED
IN YOUR REAL ESTATE CAREER

There are few enterprises which an inexperienced salesman can enter and, in a very short time, be rewarded for his efforts with such substantial financial gains. Lengthy schooling is not necessary in order to qualify as a real estate salesman. There is, however, a price you have to pay for success in this field. You will be giving up most of your evenings, many weekends and planned vacations. You will find yourself unable to make plans in advance for social activities. You will have to work hard—and think, eat and sleep real estate. *And you can find it all very worthwhile and rewarding.*

Passing the Test

When I decided that real estate was for me, all that was necessary to become a real estate salesman in my state at that time was to be sponsored by a real estate company, take a course given by any real estate company or go to a school. You could even buy the required book on your own, and take the test. If you passed the state test and applied for your license within the specified time after notification, you became a real estate salesman.

Since that time, the rules have been changed in my state. A call to your local Real Estate Commission will give you the requirements in your own state. Many states now subscribe to the "Princeton Exam." Under this plan, the prospective real estate salesman completes a course in Real Estate Principles and Practices given at an approved school. When he passes the course, he applies for the Princeton Exam. This is a 4 hour, 100 question test with questions on laws, rules and regulations, on comprehension of real estate subject matter and on math. Once he has passed this Princeton Exam, both he and the Real Estate Commission are notified. He then selects the broker in whose office he wishes to

3

become employed, fills out the required forms which his broker signs, pays the necessary fees and obtains his real estate license from the Real Estate Commission. With the receipt of his license, he becomes a full-fledged rookie.

Passing the test and obtaining the real estate license is only the beginning. It is like being newly born into an unfamiliar world—and that is exactly how you feel when you walk into your first real estate office to begin working. If selling real estate was easy, sales commissions would not be as high as they are. Thousands of real estate agents pass the test. About one-third of them quit before their first year and are replaced by other eager recruits, ready to try their hand at selling. It is generally acknowledged that approximately 10 percent of the salesmen in real estate make most of the money. The others just limp along. A rookie salesman should be constantly trying to find out how the top agents do it.

Selecting Your Broker

Select your broker with care. Real estate firms specialize and deal in one or more of the following aspects of real estate: *residential* (which includes listing and sale of townhouses, condominiums and rental properties); *commercial* (including land); *industrial;* and *investments* and *appraisals.* Since most real estate offices and their agents work mainly with the listing and selling of residential homes, most agents earn their commissions listing and selling homes. After you have been an agent for a while, you may find yourself gravitating toward one or another aspect of real estate selling. Don't try to specialize at first. If you are really good in certain areas of real estate, it will soon become apparent to your prospects and to your fellow associates, who will be glad to pass leads on to you. If you have a prospect for property in some area of real estate in which you do not specialize, don't hesitate to cooperate with another salesman who is familiar with this field. Remember, *half a commission is better than none.*

Shall it be a large real estate firm or a small one? There is something to be said for each. The "floor time" (time in the office when call-in leads go to you) you can expect to receive should influence which broker you select. A broker who is just starting in the real estate business may be willing to give you floor time all day long, but you can end up with simply that—time on the floor, but no calls. In any event, *your preference should always be a real estate company whose reputation has been established because of its integrity and good service.*

Large real estate companies have many offices and many agents.

They generally advertise more than do the smaller ones, and may have secretaries and processing departments for calls and follow-up. You may, however, be able to learn more in a small office working closely with your broker, where you are involved in all phases of real estate, must process your own cases and go to your own settlements. When you handle the entire transaction, you have a closer rapport with the buyers and the sellers and have more opportunity for recommendations and referrals from them. You learn! You make mistakes in the learning process, but learn to avoid similar ones in the future.

Franchised Brokers

The concept of franchised real estate brokers started slowly, about 1965, in the western part of the country, and by 1975, was mushrooming throughout the nation. The local broker is franchised by a home company—(Century 21, Red Carpet and Gallery of Homes, to name some of the early ones)—which supplies "brand-name" advertising in newspapers, on radio and on television, and promotional material including distinctive "For Sale" signs. Each franchised broker contributes to the advertising fund and also pays the home company a percentage of its revenues. The local broker who may operate a small company, retains his identity, but also is part of the larger corporate image and profits from the extensive advertising.

Working With Your Associates

In some real estate offices, you just jump in cold, and it's sink or swim. You can be in total confusion. A helpful sales manager will sometimes try to team up a new agent with veteran salesmen who can show him his way around. It is a good idea to select an agent who seems knowledgeable, sympathetic and helpful, and try to emulate him. Listen to the way he handles his phone inquiries and how he greets his prospects. I have seen new agents come bouncing into the office on their first day, new license in hand, ready to conquer worlds. "Look out, all you top producers" they seem to say. "Here I come to take your place, so kindly step aside and make room for me." After a few weeks of disappointments, they start to realize that it isn't going to be as easy as they thought.

With no backlog of ready prospects and referrals available, they either have to wait for the phones to ring or go out and generate their own new business. Here is my advice to rookie agents on how to best get along with their new associates:

■ *The successful real estate agent* takes pride in the office he represents and speaks well of his associates. He is always pleased when
a sale is made by any other member of his firm and is never
jealous of the success of another agent.

■ A *professional agent* never interferes when another salesman is
working with a prospect, especially if they have both just returned from inspecting houses. I have seen eager agents push
their own listings and break up an imminent sale by injecting
themselves between agent and prospect, saying: "This fantastic
listing—it's a cream puff—did you see it?" If the prospect is
already half-sold on one of the homes he has seen, he now feels
cheated unless his agent drops everything and they go out again
to see this interfering agent's "fantastic" listing, which usually
turns out to be either overpriced or cluttered and mediocre. If
the prospect is disappointed in this last house, he tends to blame
his agent and feels he was fooled about the listing. He then
starts to wonder if perhaps the agent was also wrong about the
house he has been considering. With doubts and second thoughts
will come his excuse—"I want to go home and think about it."
He may walk out feeling he made a lucky escape. This agent has
probably lost a good prospect in addition to the lost sale.

■ An *experienced agent* will never advise another salesman's prospect about any houses the prospect has already seen with his
own agent. He may have already made his decision, and you
do not want to be responsible for diverting him and preventing
a sale.

■ A *smart real estate agent* treats everyone who comes into the
office with courtesy, no matter whom he asks for, or if the prospect is rich or poor, buyer or renter. (A poor man can have rich
relatives, and a renter can become a buyer.)

■ A *cooperative agent,* answering the phone for a co-agent, never
forgets to record the date and time of the call, and to get the
correct spelling of the caller's name. The message should not
read: "Mr. Smith called. He said it was very important. Call
him as soon as you get into the office." (This was the entire
message I once received from a new agent.) If a message comes
in for an associate, the agent answering the call should make
every effort to track him down. If the call needs immediate
attention and this agent cannot be reached, he should do everything he can to help the caller.

■ A *good real estate agent* abides by all the rules set forth in his
office. He logs his prospects and clients into the daily log book

if this is a requirement. He *never* attempts to "entice" another agent's prospects. If he has just listed a house, he brings the listing into the office promptly, so that the other agents may know of its existence. He never walks around with it in his pocket hoping for his own prospect to come out and buy it—(a "pocket listing"). When he inspects a house, he makes sure that he leaves his card with the sellers or signs in, if that is requested. If he takes a key from the office to show or inspect a property, he returns it promptly.

- *An ethical real estate agent* respects another agent's listing and never "goes behind his sign" (tries to talk the sellers into listing with him before the listing has, in fact, expired). On showing a property, the agent does not attempt in any manner to undermine the rights of the listing agent:

1. He does not ask the seller why he listed with the other agent.
2. He does not imply that he and his company could do a better job if only he had the listing.
3. He does not ask when the listing is about to expire.
4. He does not answer any questions pertaining to the listing asked by the seller, but rather refers him to his own listing agent and/or company.

Women as Real Estate Agents

Women real estate agents were not always readily accepted by some buyers and sellers. At one time, many men refused to deal with a woman agent, and would specifically request a man. (Some men still do!) But women have proven themselves in this field, and do make excellent, productive agents. They understand what the woman prospect is looking for in a home, and have sympathetic understanding of the problems that may come up. Some of the largest real estate organizations in the country have found that women agents are predominant among their top producers. Some women agents have disadvantages of necessary home activities and responsibilities. Unlike men, they may have to take care of their children and be home during certain hours. They may also have to set aside time for shopping and cooking, and are frequently called upon to become the family chauffeur. However, if they can arrange their time, and their families are willing to cooperate, the monetary rewards and the satisfaction they derive, will more than compensate them. (To make things simple, the author uses "salesman" to mean a man or a woman agent, and "he" to mean "he" or "she" throughout the book.)

Floor Time

Most sales managers will team up two agents to cover given periods of time during the hours that the office remains open. This is done on a rotation schedule, and is called "floor time." (In most real estate offices, floor time is allocated to full time agents only.) Any calls and walk-in prospects are serviced by these agents on floor duty. Generally, the agents will determine how to split the proceeds between them, be it listing or selling commissions. One agent may answer the phones for the first hour, while his backup greets the walk-in prospects. The second hour they reverse roles, or they may simply rotate the calls as they come in. If there is no secretary to take messages, the agents on floor duty are responsible for doing so. Determine what your responsibilities are in relation to messages and general information calls.

Don't Discriminate

Never accept a listing until you are sure that a clear, concise and complete understanding exists between the sellers and yourself—that *the property will be offered to prospective buyers regardless of their race, color, creed or country of national origin.* Any other agreement, inferred or otherwise, is in direct violation of the law. The real estate salesman is not permitted to become a party to any decision to reject a contract offer that is based on the above. When another salesman presents a purchase offer on a home you have listed, you should *not* ask whether the buyer is black. Actually, you are better off not knowing. If the seller is reluctant to sell to a member of some minority group because of what the next-door neighbor will think, remind him that his neighbor would not ask him to break the law.

▪ BUILDING SUCCESSFUL
SALES QUALITIES

First Impressions Count

Make your first impression a favorable one. Keep your ash trays clean, your papers in order at all times and your desk clear of files. Drive a modern car and keep it neat. It's easy to accumulate maps, books, papers and candy wrappers from the children of the last family you carted around. Make it a habit to clear the car when you leave from home each morning.

Don't be concerned that friends and clients will think you are making loads of money. This is exactly the impression you want to create. Look your best and dress neatly and well, but not flamboyantly. Your public image counts. Nobody likes a loser and surely no one wants to give his business to someone who doesn't look successful. Let your friends, neighbors and relatives think you are prospering and that you have long lists of prospects and clients ready to buy and sell with just a phone call from you. Remember to always be cheerful. A smile makes you a welcome caller.

Importance of Enthusiasm

I had approached the field of real estate with such excitement and anticipation, that at first it was difficult for me to fall asleep at night. In the daytime I talked real estate with everyone I met. I read everything I could that even remotely related to the subject. When I drove around town, real estate signs on front lawns caught my eye. All night long I dreamed I was showing homes and writing offers. One day I asked the president of our company when this feeling would wear off. His answer: "After more than 20 years in the business it still hasn't for me."

This is my tenth year selling real estate and it still has the same magic and excitement for me. The phone rings and I still dash out to the office to meet a prospect or to a seller's house to list it for sale. I still get excited with the sellers when I list their home and with the buyers who are looking for a home, especially if it is to be their first. Enthusiasm is contagious. When you get excited, your prospect gets excited; the more excited he becomes, the more likely he is to buy. *Become enthusiastic and stay enthusiastic.* If you enjoy what you are doing, this enthusiasm will be genuine.

Always Be Optimistic

It is easy to get discouraged when you see your associates getting phone calls and taking prospects out, while you are just sitting, waiting. Remember—no salesman is immune from lulls in activity. Even though every step you take forward seems to be followed by two steps backward, don't allow it to get you down. Worry can make you lose your self-confidence, and then you may become insecure and depressed. No matter how bad times are, walk into the office each day with a smile and a good morning to all. Transmit optimism—keep cheerful. Let your enthusiasm and confidence radiate from you. Then when a prospect does call or come in, you will be ready for him. An enthusiastic, optimistic and cheerful attitude can spell the difference between success and failure. Get on the phone and make friendly calls. You can ask friends: "Can you do me a favor? I need some business. Do you know of anyone planning to buy or sell a home?" People love doing favors. Be sincere in your approach—you may just get a prospect or two.

When things are slow, that is the time to call all those prospects who thought that they might be looking for a house in a few months. A call or letter will require some time, but it will be time well spent. (You might as well keep active. You may turn a lull into a selling streak and surprise yourself.) Take inventory on how you have been spending your time. Have you been using it intelligently? Constructively? Now is the time to learn how to increase your personal efficiency. Sometimes, taking a short vacation can rid you of negative thoughts and you will come back refreshed, optimistic and raring to begin that selling streak.

Think "Success" and Be Aware of Opportunities

A success story is told of one real estate salesman. It seems he was such a terrible driver and his prospects were so anxious to get out of his car after inspecting several houses, that they were *ready to buy anything* once they landed. But this is only a story. There is satisfaction in success—and direct rewards *do* result. Keep your mind open to opportunities as they arise. *When you lose a single prospect through carelessness you not only lose one sale, but you lose all future referrals that would have originated with this prospect.*

Every great salesman has a need to succeed. He is so obsessed with success that he can hurdle any problems on his way. He may create the illusion that he is taking it easy all the time and working short hours, but this is only because he has developed his skill by training, experience and careful planning so that it just seems this way. Though the road to success is filled with much confusion and many disappointments, the good salesman learns to accept this and lets nothing deter him. There is no quick success. Before you can become a sales pro, you will have traveled a rough and rugged road. You cannot attain success if you program yourself for failure. Think positively and think success. You will then attain success. I know this is true. It has been working this way for me!

Use Your Imagination and Be Resourceful

To be successful and stand out from the crowd, you have to be creative and imaginative. Take advantage of opportunities as they are presented. One day, while I was driving to show a ranch style home to a prospective buyer, the man pointed to a colonial-styled house on a corner lot and said: "Now that's a lovely house." This house was the home of a family I knew would be moving in about seven or eight months. Since the prospect needed a home immediately and was willing to pay top dollar for it, I approached the homeowners and asked if they would consider moving earlier if they got a good price for their home. I worked out a deal in which I found the sellers a short-term rental and sold their home to my prospects, becoming both the lister and the seller. Everybody was delighted, including me.

Persistence

Persistence is an important asset in selling real estate. Some salesmen seem to be successful despite adversity; others may say that they are lucky, and getting all the breaks. However, attributing all success to luck does not take into account that successful salesmen refuse to accept mediocre conditions, but work to change them. They refuse to go along with the crowd accepting bad times. They spend their hours researching, and searching for the home that suits the particular needs of their prospective buyers. These agents maintain a positive attitude and work hard and persistently. Instead of sitting back and saying: "I am having a run of bad luck" and making excuses for their lack of effort, they undertake to improve themselves. They try to find out what they may have done to lose a listing or a sale. When they have a good day, they ask themselves: "What did I do different this day?" These salesmen use their creative capabilities and follow up on any prospective buyers with persistence and actually create their "luck." Their positive attitude is the answer to "times are bad—nobody is buying." Their motto is: "The harder you work, the luckier you become." If you are persistent and just "keep pitching," it will work out for the best.

Establish a Bond of Sympathy and Trust

Be honest with the buyers and the sellers you represent and they will be more than willing to work with you for the sale. Establish a bond of sympathy and trust. People are emotional about buying and

Persistence.

selling a home for many reasons. Perhaps they are on the verge of a separation or having financial difficulties, and hate the thought of moving from the area and uprooting the children. You can be the friendly advisor. If they seem unhappy, remember that you are not really the target for other people's unhappiness. If people did not have problems, they would not be coming to you for your help. Sellers and buyers often get the pre-settlement jitters. Some may call you each day after the contract is accepted and finalized. Many times, the call is only to "touch base" and to ask a trivial question. Be sympathetic, it is just a bid for reassurance.

Read About Real Estate

Read magazines, books, pamphlets, circulars, newspapers and newsletters. Keep up with what's happening in the field of real estate. Your local Real Estate Board sponsors sales conferences and seminars. Attend all your office sales meetings. Get to know all the listings of homes currently on the market and the new ones as they are brought in.

Familiarize yourself with all the printed forms in your office (listings, contract offers, leases, releases, etc.). Remember the wise old saying: *"The big print giveth while the little print taketh away."* Don't assume that something is covered in the contract offer; make sure it is, and that you know which paragraph covers it should a question arise. (Unless you have an amazing memory, write down what you learn, and file it where you can find it.)

Take Self-Inventory

A professional agent never stops evaluating himself. He considers himself a professional in a business dedicated to the premise that the sale itself is never as important as the result of the sale. If you know and understand yourself, you will be able to know and understand others. When you learn your own weaknesses and limitations and discover your own strengths, you can better understand those in the people you will be working with in real estate, because real estate is a "people business." Discipline yourself. Don't just coast along. Don't be a run-of-the-mill salesman.

Don't Offend

Some people cannot tolerate smoke and are too polite to tell you to stop smoking. They may be in such a hurry to leave you that they will forget all about the houses they are considering. It is also a good rule never to drink on the job, even if you are offered one. Keep clear of off-color jokes or any jokes about religious or ethnic groups. Don't put political stickers on your car. You are selling houses not candidates. The people you drive around may support different candidates.

Establish Realistic Goals and Work Towards Those Goals

Good salesmen are developed, not born. In order to succeed, you have to work at it. In real estate selling, you must remember that it usually takes from 60 to 90 days (or longer) for the house you have just sold or listed to result in settlement—and you do not get your commission check until after the case has been settled and the funds disbursed. Many people who enter real estate have been accustomed to a regular weekly paycheck. No matter how little they had been previously earning, it was regular and offered a certain sense of security.

The real estate salesman must learn to live with feast or famine. He is essentially self-employed and needs great determination to succeed. I have heard some agents say: "Well, I can relax now. I just sold a house." Surely these agents have set themselves no goals at all. Make your goal a realistic one, and take every opportunity to exceed your goal. A rookie salesman may sometimes have "beginner's luck" but no one can depend on this type of luck to last.

Acquire Confidence

The selling market in real estate is highly competitive, and you cannot bluff your way through. Some agents make rash promises that are impossible to keep; thus creating problems that cause them to lose face with their clients and prospects. Never hesitate to say that you do not know the answer to a question. You can always try to find the answer—no one is expected to know everything! Make sure of the facts before you promise anything. You should be professional and knowledgeable, and with knowledge comes confidence. Once you have gained confidence in your own ability, you will be in a better position to help your clients and your prospects.

It is also important to remember that a successful salesman must be a "good closer." A good closer is one who has confidence in himself and his ability, and knows how to control his prospect to achieve the desired sale. His self-confidence inspires the confidence of his prospect. He knows that as soon as he shows indecision, his prospect will reflect that mood. A rookie and a professional salesman may spend equal amounts of time, energy and gasoline with their prospects. The difference is closing the sale, and shows up in the commission checks.

Take Advice Constructively

There is always something new to learn. When an agent thinks he already knows everything about real estate, he has closed his mind to knowledge that might lead to many additional sales opportunities. If you don't know how to handle a given situation, ask your sales manager, and then take his advice.

Keep Your Sense of Humor

It is necessary to have the right attitude to condition yourself for success. One prerequisite is a sense of humor—this is a good way to break the ice and establish rapport with your buyers and sellers. Real estate can be a "fun business." If you can ride around all day, trucking families here and there, with their sticky-fingered children waving their lollipops in and out of your hair, and can end the day with no sale and no commission, and can still go home smiling and say: "Some funny things happened today," you know you are in the right business. Remember, work is only work when you do not enjoy what you are doing. If you keep your sense of humor, you will see the amusing side of daily situations as they occur.

Showing houses.

chapter two

GOOD LISTINGS
ARE LIKE HAVING
MONEY IN THE BANK

A rookie salesman should concentrate his efforts on obtaining marketable listings. He needs to learn how to get listing leads, how to prepare for the listing appointment and how to handle the listing interview. Most importantly, he must become an expert at getting the signature on the listing agreement and then following up after the listing has been signed. He should familiarize himself with all the different types of listings available, and the workings of the multiple listing service, if such a service is available in his area. The challenge of listing homes can sharpen his mental faculties.

▪ SALEABLE LISTINGS:
THE SUBSISTENCE OF ANY
REAL ESTATE OFFICE

Most new salesmen do not fully appreciate the value of a saleable listing. *A property well listed is half sold.* Concentrate your efforts on prospecting for listings that are realistically priced and therefore marketable. Almost anyone can obtain overpriced listings, but they are not worth much. An agent may list many properties each week, but if the listings are not priced right and do not get sold, the agent does not get paid. *In order for a real estate salesman to receive his commission, the property must be sold.* Some inexperienced agents ask the seller to set his own price on his home. Then they take that figure, no matter how high, and add to it the company's commission, and use this as the selling price. Since the seller's emotions are tied up in his home, he may set a price that is much too high. It is your responsibility, as a professional real estate salesman, to discourage the seller from pricing himself out of the market. In order for the listing to be saleable, it must attract prospective purchasers and other salesmen and their buyers. It will not do so if priced too high above comparable properties. No matter who sells the house, whether the listing company or a competitive one, the lister of the property receives a commission. *If you can set a realistic price at the time you list the property, you will not only get it sold faster, but have happier clients to add to your circle of future referrals.*

One of the most important bits of information for your records is the *reason* that the seller is selling his home. You should listen carefully to determine what this reason is. If the reason is sufficiently compelling, a seller can often be induced to list his home at a price that produces a fast sale. It should be priced as close to the fair market value as possible. You should be aware throughout the listing interview that the seller is very emotional about his home (he may have spent many weekends working on that rock garden or built-in cabinet); therefore, try to be as enthusiastic as he is. The seller may lose confidence in the salesman who says that the home is not as valuable as the seller feels it is, even though the seller has set a highly inflated value.

Should you be asked to help personal friends sell their home, make sure you get it down in writing. Don't be careless because they are friends. Have the listing agreement signed by both husband and wife, so that there will be no future misunderstanding concerning the terms under which you are listing the property. One of our rookie agents brought in a listing from a couple who were his friends for years, knowing that the wife had signed for both the husband and herself. When an offer to purchase was later written, the husband refused to sell; the couple was splitting up.

If you are called to list a property and you are certain that there is no chance for it to sell under the existing conditions, never mislead the sellers. You will just be jeopardizing your own reputation when it does not sell and be wasting time and energy in addition. A case in point: I was once called in to list a property. The sellers wanted $25,000 for a run-down house that would need at least $2,000 for repairs and cleanup. This house had a first mortgage of $18,000 and someone had foolishly given them a second mortgage for $5,000 on the property. Similar homes in the area, in excellent condition, were selling for $19,000. I felt sorry for these people but had to tell them I could offer them no help.

When you take an unsaleable listing for the "thrill" of bringing a listing into the office, you will soon regret it. Phone calls from the anxious sellers every few days, wanting to know why the house is not being shown and why it has not been sold, convince you that you should pass by unsaleable listings.

■ DIFFERENT TYPES OF LISTINGS

A homeowner who wishes to be represented by a real estate company is required to sign a listing form authorizing the company to make every effort to obtain a qualified buyer for his home. The company assists in getting the financing and tries to make the process as easy as possible for the seller's peace of mind and comfort. There are various types of listings.

Exclusive Right of Sale

This is the most common form of listing. The exclusive right of sale gives the broker an exclusive right to sell the property during a specified period written into the listing form. Should he, any other broker or the seller himself produce a buyer interested in purchasing the property during this listing time, the listing broker is entitled to his commission. With this type of listing, the seller gets preferred attention and the property is generally advertised.

Exclusive Agency Listing

Sometimes a homeowner will give his listing to a real estate company only if he, the seller, is permitted to sell his property by himself during the same period—in this case he need not pay any commission to the listing company. The listing company, however, has the exclusive agency right and should another real estate company make the sale, the listing broker gets the commission.

There are reasons why this type of listing is undesirable. Complications arise when an owner advertises the sale of his home in the very same paper in which the listing company is running a similar advertisement. (His ad may even appear directly above or below the company ad.) The descriptions are exactly the same but the asking price in the owner ad is less than the price the real estate company has advertised. Also, the homeowner's price is generally negotiable.

Sometimes a seller will request that his home be listed as "exclusive agency" for his own personal reasons. He may want your sign placed on his front lawn immediately because he has a "hot prospect" and is trying to bargain with him for a higher selling price. He can then show this prospect your company sign and the listing in which the price is set higher than the one he is quoting. However, don't refuse to take an exclusive agency listing. Usually in a few weeks, the seller tires of trying to sell his house by himself, and will convert the listing to an exclusive right of sale.

Open Listings

An open listing is one which is given to one or more real estate companies in the vicinity, without any having the exclusive right to sell. Whichever real estate company produces the buyer, that is the company that earns the commission. (The seller should be made to realize that one broker, working exclusively in the interest of his client, the seller, can do a better job than a dozen agents working halfheartedly.) There are many disadvantages to the agent and his company in this type of listing. One real estate company may be spending money on advertising the house, while another company may be busy selling it, and a third in the process of writing a contract offer. You might show a house so listed to an interested prospect who is ready to buy, only to find that the house was sold by another real estate company on the previous day.

Contingency Listings

Sometimes a homeowner will call your office, asking for an agent to come out—he is thinking of selling his home. When you get there, you find out that that is exactly what he is doing—*thinking* of selling his home. He has not yet received his transfer notice, nor his job offer. Or he may be thinking of moving closer to his place of business and hasn't started looking for his new home yet. Whatever the reason, if you feel that he is serious (and not seeking a free appraisal on his home) you can still write a listing "contingent on seller receiving a job transfer notice by a certain date" or to "coincide with settlement on new home," etc. There are buyers who will accept these terms. If a prospect has been looking for a home such as you have listed and he is in no immediate hurry (for example, he is currently on a month-to-month rental basis in an apartment) he may accept these terms. Then when the sellers finalize their transfer, you can remove any contingency on the contract and you have made a sale.

The Net Listing

Few real estate practices have been as generally condemned by authorities in the field of real estate, as has the practice of net listing. A net listing is a listing in which the seller is to receive a stated dollar amount if the property is sold. A broker is free to offer the property for sale at any higher price and if sold, the broker only pays the seller the net amount agreed upon in the listing, retaining the difference as his commission. The danger to the unsophisticated seller is apparent. Where the normal listing agreement specifies the commission as a percentage of the selling price of the property (i.e., 5%, 6%, 7%, etc.) and offers every incentive to the broker to list at the highest marketable price, the opposite may be true for a net listing. In such a listing, the greater the difference between the amount of the net listing and the selling price, the greater the broker's commission.

The "Any Way You Can Get It" Listing

If you have a prospect for a particular house that is not currently on the market, make every effort to get this type of house listed. You can call people who are currently occupying this type of home, explaining your need. Perhaps they have been contemplating a move. A ready buyer may help them make a decision to sell now. A homeowner may have been advertising his home "For Sale by Owner" and had no luck with his ad. He may welcome your offer of a "one day listing and showing appointment." (Even if your prospect does not buy his home, he may become so impressed with your know-how that he will call on you to list his home when the ad runs out.)

You may receive a phone call from the sellers of a property that was once listed with another company. They are unhappy with their agent and his company and would like you to come out and help them sell their home. Always be ethical in your dealings. Make sure that the listing has, in fact, expired. Then go to work. If the listing with the other company is still in effect, thank them for calling you but explain that it is not ethical for you to be talking with them about listing their home at this time; that when their current listing expires, should the house still remain unsold, you will be delighted to do everything you can to help sell the house.

Of course, there is always one sure way to get a listing. You can buy the house yourself. I am not being funny. The following actually happened. When we first opened our real estate branch office, we had no listings at all. In order to attract prospects, it was necessary to have at least one house listed that we could advertise, so our company president, together with our sales manager, started reading "For Sale by Owner" ads themselves, looking for a bargain to buy. They finally decided on one. It was a run-down house with possibilities and was bought cheaply by the company. The sellers were a couple who had recently separated and left the premises. We could now advertise:

BARGAIN—NEEDS TENDER LOVING CARE

The house needed plenty of that! The company fixed it up somewhat and decided to hold it "open" the following Sunday. The ad was placed in our local papers. The house was then swept clean and a bathroom door with a large fist hole in the center, removed and hidden in the garage. We held it open Sunday after Sunday. It took a long time to sell but was a great help to all of the agents. Whenever we wanted to insure a sale, we showed this house first. Any other one looked GREAT by comparison.

▪ THE MULTIPLE
LISTING SERVICE (MLS)

Many local Real Estate Boards have a central clearing house where exclusive listings for the sale or lease of real estate are submitted by member brokers, for distribution to other brokers. The Multiple Listing Service (MLS) is one of several such cooperative methods offered. To some REALTORS it is still a relatively new experience, but it is one that has been used in my area. It is basically a method of handling the clerical processing of listings in a central location. These listings, when received by the MLS, are printed and distributed to participating brokers for cooperative selling. In this way, a client of a member REALTOR is assured his property will receive wide market exposure. Although some real estate firms do not subscribe to this service but instead cooperate on their listings, more and more companies are gradually taking advantage of the system and becoming a part of it. The public relations value of the MLS has proven effective and once the broker has negotiated an exclusive listing, the physical process of getting all the information to the other cooperating brokers is accomplished very efficiently.

MLS offers many services to both buyers and sellers of real estate.

"All it needs is tender, loving care."

The sellers have wider coverage for the sale of their homes and the buyers are advised that when they come into your office (and you are a subscribing member of the service) they need go no further, since you can advise them of all the homes currently listed in the area no matter who has the listing.

MLS does, however, differ from area to area—each Board has its own procedures. In one area, sheets containing listing information are distributed each day (called "dot sheets"). These are sent out two days after the listing is submitted. It contains no house picture at this time, but is in MLS number sequence. Two days later, it is again sent out in the form of a card, with the picture of the house. A disposition sheet is sent along, which contains all the data submitted and shows what has been sold, the selling price, the method of financing and any listing changes.

A number of years ago, before the multiple listing service had been introduced into our office, local brokers cooperated with each other and distributed information on their individual listings. If our office did not have a listing on a particular property that one of our prospects was seeking, we would look for one possibly listed with a cooperating broker. It was necessary to phone each broker asking if such a listing had recently come in, and attempt to get an agent who was not busy doing his own work, to read the listing to you. It was time-consuming getting the details. You might be kept on "hold" while the agent at the other end went to search it out. Or you might be asked to "please call back later—all my phones are ringing." Meanwhile, the prospect waited impatiently. Many times the phones in our office would be ringing continuously with similar requests after our office had obtained a well-priced listing.

When the multiple listing service was introduced into our office, all the agents sighed in relief. We gladly filled in the required listing form, mailed it to the MLS office where it was duplicated and printed up with a picture of the house being offered for sale. This was a great improvement over the old co-op system, since all the information needed was printed on the sheet received for each new listing. The picture was a great help even though, at first, the wrong one was sometimes printed. However, it did not eliminate all problems and most agents were not sure that they did not prefer the old co-op system. The MLS slips were delivered to our office each Thursday afternoon and came in a large brown grocery bag. Since delivery was once a week, only the listing office knew of their own particular listings for the first few days. Agents were again busy on the phones each morning with the old request: "Any new listings come in since Thursday?" This became so annoying that the brokers assigned one agent in each office to make the call for the day. This helped some.

Each paper bag delivered from MLS contained many individual packs of MLS slips; each about one to two inches thick and bound with rubber bands. Each pack was of one listing. If you happened to be on floor duty when the bag was delivered, you spent your entire floor time around the library table, playing "musical listings" while collating and sorting piles of listings, making sets to be placed into each agent's mail box. Sometimes the packs were delivered short. Sometimes the office phones would ring while we were collating the listings and when we got back to the table, it was hard to remember just where we had left off. As a result, not all the agents received complete sets of listings each week. Some agents did not play fair. When the listings were delivered during their floor time, they would hide the paper bag. It would appear mysteriously just as they went off floor duty, for the next agent to collate and distribute.

Introducing the Computer

The Multiple Listing Service in our area next introduced the computer. With the computer, subscribing brokers now have a terminal installed in each of their offices. This terminal looks like an oversized electric typewriter, the difference being that it types back an answer to your request. If you feed it the wrong information, it will let you know that you have made an error, in no uncertain terms. When an agent brings a new listing into the office, he fills out a "profile sheet." The instructions are clear and simple. He feeds this information into the computer (which remembers *everything*) and "voila"—any cooperating broker has immediate access to this listing information at any time. (A change of status concerning this listing is fed into the computer in the same way.) The computer makes it easy for any agent to retrieve all the pertinent facts and features of a particular home, since each listing is assigned a MLS number. When a prospect walks into our office seeking a house in a given area and the agent cannot find such a listing in his current files, he goes to the computer terminal, feeds in his request for this particular type of house and is immediately given the required information for all listings stored in the computer.

The computer has many other uses. In addition to recording the listings, it helps you search for them by features or street address. It helps you find comparables (other properties with similar features) that have sold during the last year so that you can compare their prices with the one you are trying to list or sell. This is an excellent listing and selling tool. It allows you to change the status of a current listing by taking the house off the market. You can enter a change in the expiration date of a listing or just advise of a pending sale, open house, price change or general availability.

The computer also prints out an amortization schedule if you so request, showing the principal and interest for payments in periodic amounts until the total amount has been paid. It can aid in your selling close by advising how much the prospective buyer may be losing by renting a house as against buying one, by simply feeding in information of the prospect's current earnings and current rent. Generally, each office takes a daily read-out of the current listings and changes and updates the current file cards where a property is shown as sold or taken off the market, or where the listing has expired. Changes as to price or status are also noted.

Actually, the computer terminal is capable of doing even more than this, including some of the accounting and other management functions. At this time in my area, they are testing portable terminals, smaller than an attache case, weighing less than three pounds, with the same capability as the office terminal. The agent can bring this computer to the prospect or seller and phone in from a phone booth, his car or the customer's home, with his request for information, and get a legible tape print-out with the information he requested. We all miss the individual listing slips (with pictures of the houses printed in the center) that were delivered in those brown paper bags, But with our computer terminal working, we have finally been able to relegate the library table back to the conference room, where it fits very nicely.

■ HOW TO GET THE LISTING LEADS

All You Have To Do Is Knock On Doors!

The day after passing the real estate exam, I arrived at the office bright and early, ready to start making all that money I had heard about. After being introduced to twenty or so new associates in the office, the sales manager called a meeting. He talked to us briefly. One of the things he said left a lasting impression: "To make it big in real estate, all you have to do is knock on some doors!"

Then he handed each one of us a local telephone directory, pointed out a desk and telephone for each to use and said:

> Call everybody in the telephone book. You never know who is about to move and needs your help. Call all the people you know. Tell everyone you meet that you are a real estate agent. Give out cards. *Knock on doors.* There is a good chance that one of the people you approach is planning a change.

It sounded so easy. Twenty agents opened twenty telephone books and started dialing. Since we were all calling the same people (we had all opened to the first page and the letter "A") we mostly got busy signals, but I did manage to get through to some families unfortunate enough to have been listed in the first pages of the directory.

Basically, the advice given to us by our sales manager was excellent. Being inexperienced at the time, we didn't really appreciate it. But we learned to keep busy when there was a lull in selling. Also, we learned to accept the word NO impersonally and the slammed down phone without shock. In this way we gained confidence and experience. Since those early days, I have learned to call complete strangers without qualms, knowing that I have something of value to offer. I have learned to knock on doors and start conversations in the restaurant or while waiting in line, anywhere. Although I grew up shy and retiring, now I don't close my mouth except to eat.

Call-in Listings

The easiest way to get a listing, is to be lucky on your floor time and have someone with a house to sell, walk in or call in. Take all the floor time your broker offers you. A homeowner may call for general information and if you are helpful, you may end up with a listing and/or a referral commission.

One day, while on floor duty, a man called in, and asked if I could help him locate a real estate company in a small town in another state. He was anticipating a job transfer in a few months and wanted to know what was available in homes there and their price range. I wrote down his name, address and phone number and his requirements as to rooms, etc. I told him I would check this out and get back in touch with him. I then made some phone calls directly to that area, located a REALTOR, and told him what I was looking for. He gladly sent me literature and prices on the homes available. I, in turn, delivered this to my caller's

"Yes, I'm in real estate."

home. Result: He set up an appointment with one of their agents, was delighted with the home they found for him, and gratefully listed his home with me for sale. (Since then, our company subscribes to a find-a-home service and when we refer a prospect to them, we get a commission should the prospect purchase a home as a result of our efforts.)

It may seem, at times, that all the call-ins come when your lucky associates have floor duty. Don't be discouraged. The law of averages works and you will get your share. Also remember, *not every call-in inquiry results in a listing!* When a homeowner calls the office and says: "Can you come right out, I am thinking of selling my home," don't start calculating your commission yet. You don't know for sure how many real estate companies he has already called and how many agents have been there. You don't know if the seller is really serious about selling or just wants a real estate salesman's reassurance that his home has increased in value. Perhaps a woman who calls is a little bored today and wants to show off the slip covers she has just completed or wants someone to talk with while the children are napping. If the homeowner is in fact serious about selling and you can convince him of your ability and your know-how, you may walk out with a listing. There is no way of knowing in advance whether you will be wasting your time or not.

One day I received a phone call from a woman living in a nearby apartment house complex. She told me she owned a small house near our office that she was thinking of selling and asked if I would look at it from the outside (it was tenant occupied) and come over that evening to give her my opinion as to its value and saleability. When I knocked on her door at the appointed time, I was invited in and asked if I would have any objections to a neighbor dropping in. I thought this an unusual request (people are generally private about selling their homes) but I said it would be all right. Before I had my coat off, there was a knock on the door and the neighbor came in. Something didn't feel quite right. This neighbor listened to every word I said. It didn't take long for me to figure out what it was all about. Mrs. Homeowner was trying to sell her home to this neighbor. They were unable to come to terms on the price and I had been called in to help determine it for them. Realizing this, and becoming annoyed because I had just wasted an evening, my gas, etc., I set such a high price on the house that this neighbor nearly fell out of the chair. Then smiling sweetly, I said "good night" and left.

The following sounded like a bona fide listing call, until I got there:

Caller: Hello, may I speak with a knowledgeable real estate agent?

Me: May I help you? My name is Charlotte Korn. With whom am I speaking?

Caller: My name is Mr. Johnson. I have this ranch style house, which I have been living in for the past three years. I was thinking of selling it. Can you come right out?

(Finally, a real, live listing call?) I wrote down the man's name, address and phone number. Then I did some lightning research and took off. It was a lovely home, and in excellent condition both inside and out. And he was selling it. *But to a relative.* He was not sure how much to ask for it and needed a fast appraisal, and "thank you very much for coming out and being so helpful!" Oh, well. . . .

Soliciting (Cold Canvassing)

I first started in real estate in a newly opened branch office, staffed with agents who, like myself, had just passed the real estate exam and were raring to go. Our office was situated between a furniture store on the left and a pet store on the right. Since we were not yet listed in the local telephone directory, nor had a sign over the store window, the agents had to verify the address just to make sure they were coming to work to the right place! We did, however, have a lovely lamp in the window and it attracted attention. People came in all the time thinking we were part of the furniture store. They all wanted to know the price of the lamp in the window. We really didn't care what brought them in. Once in, we sat them down, asked them how they liked their coffee and tried to sell them a house.

When this furniture store vacated, a delicatessen store opened in its place. Since people do have to eat and our new sign now blazed above our door, we anticipated hungry homebuyers and sellers dropping in. A car would pull up. The agent on floor duty would look hopefully at the people coming out of the car, but the couple with the cute puppy went into the pet store and the lean, hungry ones turned to the delicatessen. We soon learned that a real estate salesman could not count on walk-ins alone for his prospects. He could not be content to sit and *wait for things to happen to him.* He would have to *make them happen for him.* We quickly learned to:

- Drive around looking for signs that appeared on front lawns proclaiming that the house was "For Sale by Owner"; note the phone number and address and rush back to the office in order to start dialing for an appointment.

- Knock on the doors of homes on either side of a home being offered for sale or already sold by a real estate company, preferably our own, and ask if they knew someone planning to move into the area, or if they were themselves planning to move in the future.

- "Cold canvass" from the telephone directory by asking: "Mrs. Homeowner, could you do me a favor? I am looking for a home for an anxious buyer who loves the street where you live. Do you know of anyone planning to move?"

- Check news items such as military transfers, promotions, divorces and marriages, etc.

- Ask everyone we met—the mailman, milkman, gasoline attendant, grocery clerk, etc., if they could recommend any business to us. We let them all know we were anxious to serve. We gave out cards to all saying: "I have to give out my quota of cards each day," and smiled. (I even picked up a listing client while waiting in the drugstore for my prescription to be filled!)

Calling "For Sale by Owner" Ads

Many agents are timid about calling an owner who has advertised his home for sale in the papers. They are afraid of being rejected and cannot accept the word "NO."

When our office first opened, and we had little referral business, we were told by our sales manager that we could either keep a seat warm and earn nothing, or we could use our time learning the business and attempting to solicit listings. We turned to the local papers and the "For Sale by Owner" ads. If a homeowner ran an ad, he was immediately besieged by all of our twenty eager beavers (in addition to many agents from other real estate companies in the area). While Mr. Homeowner was waiting for his phone to ring and a rush of home buyers to beat a path to his door, droves of eager salesmen descended on him instead. After being polite to the first ten callers and explaining that he was selling his home himself to save the commission, his patience would become exhausted and he'd be ready to "blast" the next agent who called. I learned a valuable lesson during this period. *In order to beat the competition,* I would have to *offer something different* or *better* than any other agent, or I would have to get there first. Since I could not always be the first to get there, I concentrated on discovering that "something different." I already knew that though *many agents may call on the homeowner* who has advertised his home for sale, *only a few manage to get into the house* and *only one* comes away with the listing. I decided that the first step would be to get into the house.

Getting Your Foot in the Door

The first homeowner I ever listed had been running an ad in the local paper for some time. Almost every agent in our office had been trying to get an appointment but I was unaware of this at the time I phoned. I read the ad with a funny feeling in the pit of my stomach and gathered up enough courage to dial the number listed. A woman answered and I told her that I was a real estate agent and gave her the name of my company. I asked if I could come over to see her home and talk about selling it. I tried to sound helpful. When she set up an appointment for that evening I could hardly believe my luck and told everyone in the office about it.

I drove up early and sat outside in the car until the exact minute of the appointed time, and then knocked timidly at the door and was invited into the house. Around the kitchen table sat Mr. and Mrs. Homeowner and a well-dressed young man, his papers spread out in front of him. I apologized for intruding but was assured that "the gentleman is just leaving." On hearing this, he quietly gathered up his papers, stuffed them into his briefcase and left. I was invited to sit down in his place. When I looked inquiringly after the man who was leaving, the woman said: "He came here under false pretenses." She then told me that this agent had originally phoned to see the house saying he was interested in buying and never mentioned that he was a real estate agent trying to list her home for sale. When I had called, they liked my sincerity. I told the sellers that I was a new agent and that this was actually the first call I had ever made on a homeowner. They immediately put me at ease. The man was a lawyer and even helped me to fill out the listing form. I learned a valuable lesson which has been confirmed many times since that memorable day:

Honesty in real estate is one of your best listing tools.

Many agents find it difficult to list the homeowner who has advertised the sale of his home. They are afraid of being rejected. It is understandable that a homeowner who is trying to save the commission and has placed his ad in the newspapers does not want his phone tied up by agents who are trying to "take this commission away from him." However, a call to this type of owner is easier to make with practice. After all, the irate homeowner is at the other end of a telephone line and quite a distance from you. He can't even see you. The worst thing he can do is to say "NO" and bang the receiver. He thinks he knows something about selling homes and doesn't want anyone bothering him. You will just have to convince him that you know more than he does. Perhaps he may actually be seeking help and has run the ad because he didn't know what else to do. If he sounds unhappy, it may be that he resents having to leave the area and is over-anxious about moving. You must sound confident when you call. *You are helping him.* You are helping him not only to sell his home, but to get a good price for it; to relieve him of the necessity of waiting at home for the phone to ring and buyers to show up; to qualify a prospective buyer and arrange financing and to prevent him from making costly mistakes. Once you get an appointment, the hardest part is over.

Door Openers That Work

The following are some of the door openers that I have been using, and that work for me:

Hello, is this 222-3333? I am calling in answer to your ad in today's paper. My name is Charlotte Korn and I am with P.G.P. Realtors, your local real estate company here in the area. I know you must be getting many calls from real estate agents who are all trying to list your home. I also realize that you would like to sell it yourself. I hope that you are successful. *(At this point I have told the seller what he had been waiting to tell me, and I have his attention.)* I wonder if I may see your home? I have many prospects looking for homes such as you describe in your ad, and I am sure it is lovely. *(He may just be waiting to tell someone all about the room he has paneled, or the attic he floored.)* Perhaps I can be of help to you if you do find a buyer on your own. I can assist you with advice on qualifying the buyer and arranging financing. *(He never gave a thought to the need for qualifying a buyer or obtaining financing.)* Should you later decide to call in a real estate company, I would appreciate an opportunity to come by and explain all of our services to you. You will, of course, be under no obligations when I do come to your home. When may be convenient? *(If you get no appointment at this time, remember that an owner who has made the decision to advertise on his own, or place a sign on his lawn, will generally not list with any REALTOR for at least 48 hours—male ego?—so be sure you maintain your contact with him for longer than that. Try again in a few days, as follows):*

Hello. This is Charlotte Korn. I spoke with you a few days ago about the home you are offering for sale. I just thought I'd call to see how you are getting on with your ad. Have you had many inquiries? Is there anything I can do to help? May I come by this evening?

If a house has recently been sold by myself or another agent of our company, I call on the immediate neighbors, as follows:

Good afternoon. I am Charlotte Korn with P.G.P. We have just been successful in selling the home of your next door neighbor. You probably saw our sign on the James' property. May I leave my card with you? On the back I have noted that a family will probably be moving in within three weeks. They have two lovely children—a boy and a girl. Would you make them welcome? Then I add: Incidentally, do you know of anyone else who is planning to move? I would appreciate your calling me if you do. My name and phone number are right on the card. Thank you.

Good afternoon. I am Charlotte Korn. Our office, P.G.P. Realtors, has just sold the James' home right on this street. We have many prospective buyers who inspected this home when it was being offered for sale and who would like to locate in this neighborhood. Would you perhaps know of anyone planning to move in the near future?

Getting Listing Referrals

It is most important that you build up a referral system. Cultivate the people who are your happy, satisfied homeowners, who remember the transaction as a pleasant experience. Make friends with them. Drop in to see how they are getting on. Phone them and write to them. Prove by your actions that you are interested in their general welfare and they will become your "circle of referrals."

If you sold a home to a family who was transferred to your area, and if this family is pleased with the way the sale was handled and with your follow-up, you can be sure that they will be sending their friends to you as they are transferred into town. If you sold a home for a family who were leaving town and they were happy because of the service they received from you, you may be called six months later to list a home on the same street, because they were told "you must call this agent if you ever want to sell your home." The listings and prospects you get from such clients will be the easier ones. An unhappy homeowner will not go out of his way to tell his friends and neighbors to call on you with housing needs. *The building blocks of your referral system are no more than your satisfied customers.*

Landlords As Potential Listers

The field of residential real estate encompasses more than the buying and selling of homes. It includes the listing of rental property, the writing of leases, the qualifying of tenants and the follow-up. Some agents will avoid handling rental property because there is little compensation for much work. I have found this field an excellent source of additional sales commissions, referrals and friends. Sometimes, for personal reasons, the owner of a property decides he would rather rent his home than sell it. He may be leaving the area for a limited time only and wish to return to the home he loves. He may be moving to an area where he will rent a home and not need the proceeds from a sale of his present home. All of this is subject to change. He may later decide that he loves where he has moved and wouldn't think of returning to his former home. He may also feel that should he return, he would want a different style of home or neighborhood. After a short while, he may find his dream house there and decide to buy it, and will need to sell his house to raise the funds. You are his out-of-town contact and he will call on you to act for him in the sale of his home.

It is true that there may be as much work, or more, for the agent who writes up a rental listing or lease form as there is in the writing of a listing and contract offer of sale. The agent has to inspect the property and act for an absentee landlord in many instances. He has to put up a sign on the property and order a credit report on the prospective tenant. He has to present the lease for acceptance and sometimes arrange for the utilities to be transferred into the name of the tenant. He may have to assume responsibility for accepting the rent and escrow for the rental, and his total commission is negligible. However, the agent who shies away from this field is making a big mistake. He should remember that the *landlord of today is the seller of tomorrow.* That the tenant for whom he has just written a year's lease may decide to buy a home in the near future; perhaps the one he is renting. If both the landlord and the tenant are happy with your services, you have added potential buyers and sellers to your future "circle of referrals."

Listing Properties Other Than Residential Homes

From time to time, you may be called on to list property with which you have had no previous experience. Don't be afraid to do so; simply ask an associate who is an expert in this particular property type to go with you and share the listing. In this way, you will see how an expert does it and can expand your real estate opportunities. I have listed commercial properties and small retail stores. I have also listed apartment houses in this way. A split commission is better than none!

Listing Land

Location is the single most important word in real estate. Its importance cannot be overemphasized. Everything else can be changed but land is fixed. The price and terms can be negotiated and the home altered and improved, but the location always remains the same.

Raw land needs to be developed in order for its value to increase. Selling raw land is a challenge—full of opportunities for the developer who understands how to develop its potential and the salesman who knows how to sell it. Whether a small parcel or an acreage, you must know as much as possible about the value and use of the land you are listing, in order to be successful in its sale. If the parcel of land is in a residential area and is to be sold for that purpose, you will want to know its exact size, existing easements if any, if there are gas or electric services available and if there is no sewer service, the nature of the soil.

A woman walked into our office one day, and listed a $900 lot for sale with one of our agents. It was way out in the "boondocks" but at that time we were all so desperate, that any kind of business looked good. The agent went out with her sign, and after a two hour trek, finally located the lot, hammered her sign into the ground and returned. A contract offer was brought in a few days later. The purchaser had inserted the following clause into the contract offer:

This sale is subject to the land passing a perk test.

None of the other agents was exactly sure what a perk test was, but we all soon learned. Before you can build on a parcel of land where there is no existing sewer system and where a septic system is required, the land must have good drainage and "perk." To determine this, the agent went back, dug a hole the required depth, filled it with water and after the required number of days returned. The hole was still filled with water. It had not drained down at all. The buyer then requested a release from the contract.

Listing Condominiums

The word "condominium" describes a form of ownership. Condominium ownership is individual ownership in a high rise apartment, townhouse, detached house or business office. It involves ownership of a single unit in a multi-unit building or development together with ownership of a pro-rata interest in the external property which is owned and shared in common with other unit owners. The common areas usually consist of the land, yard, parking areas, playgrounds, recreation facilities, hallways, stairways, storage spaces, roof, foundation, elevators and entrances, as well as heating, air conditioning and plumbing systems. The owner of a condominium unit can be treated, for purposes of listing, as the owner of a single family house. He is permitted to sell, mortgage or otherwise transfer his rights (which include his pro-rata share of the common property) just as the owner of any other real property might do. He has his own mortgage and pays his own real estate taxes, treating mortgage interest and real estate taxes as deductible on his income tax return. He is not responsible for any default by any other unit owner in the same building.

There are some definite advantages of condominium ownership. An owner may enjoy the swimming pool, tennis courts and other recreational facilities without being concerned about maintenance and lawn care. Be sure you mention all the amenities in your listing. A condominium owner cannot separate his interest in the common properties. He must abide by the bylaws of the condominium owners' association, and pay his pro-rata share of common expenses, usually in the form of a monthly condominium fee. This fee covers the cost of maintaining the common grounds and usually includes liability insurance; it often includes utilities, sewage costs and garbage collection. The monthly condo fee should be specified in the listing. If this fee is not paid, it becomes a lien against the property.

In addition to residential apartments, condominium ownership is popular in resort areas where the owners can enjoy their pro-rata ownership in golf courses, lakes, ski slopes, etc. The condominium ownership also is used in some commercial buildings. For example, doctors or lawyers may each own their own individual office spaces, but have the advantage of common laboratories or libraries. Here again, each owner is free to transfer his own unit, subject to the purchaser abiding by the condominium bylaws (which include provisions for the monthly condo fee). Note that condominium ownership is different from cooperative ownership (co-op). In a co-op, all the owners as a group own the entire building, generally through a corporation, each owner having shares of corporate stock in proportion to the value of his unit. The mortgage covers the entire property. Since all expenses and mortgage payments in a co-op are shared, if one owner defaults, all the other co-op owners will suffer, as their corporation is liable. Unlike a condominium unit, if a co-op owner wishes to renovate his own unit, it would first have to be approved by the co-op corporation. (If he redecorates in poor taste and later defaults, the owners of the other units will have to bear the cost of redecorating again.)

■ HOW TO PREPARE FOR THE LISTING APPOINTMENT

Once you are successful in setting up the listing appointment, it is worthwhile preparing for it in advance. Following are some of the preparations I have learned to make.

.Verify That Both Husband and Wife Will Be Home

A listing is not a valid one unless signed by both husband and wife. Perhaps the husband and his wife are not getting along and only the wife wants to sell. She may sign willingly only to have the husband refuse to even talk with you. You may spend hours explaining everything to the wife in the afternoon only to have to repeat it all when the husband comes home at night. A wife, bored by this re-run, may become negative. Even where you have managed to impress the wife and she thought you were "the greatest agent in town," her husband may automatically reject you as the person to sell the house because he has a low opinion of his wife's judgment.

Do Your Research

Before you go out on that listing appointment, be sure you have done in advance, all the necessary *research on the house you expect to list.* In our area, we have a service that publishes reports showing:

- Date of purchase of each home sold.
- The amount that was paid for the home sold.
- The legal description.
- The mortgage amount at time of purchase and the interest rate.
- Who held the mortgage when the house was sold and the terms under which the house sold (VA, FHA, conventional or assumption).

Always fill out the listing form with as much advance information as you are able to obtain (from your conversation with the owner and from office reports as above—i.e., name, address, lot and block, number of rooms, appliances, etc.). When you come prepared with all this knowledge, the homeowner is quite impressed. It also helps you set the terms for the sale of the property. Where you have ascertained that the loan can be assumed and that it carries an excellent rate of interest, you know that it will be more desirable and therefore more saleable; thus you may be able to set a higher figure as the selling price.

Be Sure To Carry An Exhibit Book

Buy a large looseleaf book containing plastic insert sheets—a book that can be used for exhibit purposes. You will want to display your company's past achievements as well as your own in this book. Include a day's sample advertising to show how extensively your company advertises. Show ads of other real estate companies alongside your company's ads, so that you can point out the difference in quantity and quality. Enclose a list of the homes in the neighborhood that were personally sold by yourself or your company within the past six months, showing the prices that were asked, sales prices and information about how long they actually took to sell. It is all very impressive.

Listing Aids to Take Along

You should have the following with you when you go to list a house:

1 ▪ A list of comparable homes that are currently on the market, together with their asking prices and terms and information about how long they have been for sale.

2 ▪ A list of comparable homes that have been sold in the past six months, how they were sold, the asking prices and what they were actually sold for. (This list will include homes sold by all the brokers in the area.) If there had been any FHA or VA appraisals, take these along with you.

As you drive up for the listing appointment, note:

1 ▪ The condition of the neighborhood.

2 ▪ The proximity to schools, shopping, parks, etc.

3 ▪ The exterior condition and general appearance of the house. Does the trim need painting? Does the lawn need cutting? Are there storm windows and doors, screens, gutters? Make a mental note of all of it.

4 ■ Look for something attractive that you can comment on favorably when you first meet the sellers.

5 ■ *Above all, be on time for that appointment!*

If the appointment has been set for the evening and it will be dark when you arrive, drive out in the daytime and "just look around." The sellers are favorably impressed when they start to describe the exterior of the home and you tell them you have already been out looking around.

Re: Company Sign On Your Car

Most real estate companies require each agent to attach a sign with the company name to his car, so that people seeing these cars drive by will think: "My, what an active office that is, with so many agents driving clients and prospects around and selling homes all day long." They don't have to know that these same agents may be driving the children to the dentist, going shopping or just inspecting homes. It makes the company look good. I have a sign on my car. When I have an appointment to see a homeowner who has been advertising on his own, I am not anxious to tip off every other agent hot on the trail. I either park a few doors away from the home I am trying to list, or remove the sign from the car temporarily. There are other reasons why I prefer not to drive right up to the house I will be listing, with the company sign on the car. The family I am visiting may not be sure of their transfer and perhaps do not want the neighbors to know that they are contemplating a move. Or it may be known among the neighbors that they have been having family difficulties and they would not want the neighbors to realize that they have finally come to a parting of the ways. However, abide by your own company's policy with relation to signs on your car.

■ HOW TO HANDLE
THE LISTING INTERVIEW

Sell Yourself and Your Company to the Homeowner

The agent has to understand the homeowner's motives. The homeowner who places an ad in the papers for the sale of his own home, is doing so to save the commission. He sincerely believes he can do the job or he thinks it is a great challenge. He does not want salesmen bothering him once he has placed his ad. He doesn't want his phone tied up with salesmen's calls while he is waiting for prospects to call.

The homeowner who phones one or more real estate companies to get information about selling his home, may be thinking of either selling it himself or of giving it to the real estate company which, he feels, will do the best job for him. In order to convince the homeowner to list with you and your company, you have to show him that *it is to his benefit and advantage* to do so. You cannot bluff your way through. Neither can you be meek and retiring. You need to develop an individual style which gets across to the homeowner that you are honest, sincere, helpful, hardworking, and *know what you are talking about;* that your company is the best one to sell his home and that you will try to get him the highest available price. If you can do this the battle is half won.

Be sincere in your desire to help the homeowner whether you think you will eventually get the listing or not. Sometimes a seller who had previously thought of selling his home on his own, may decide after talking with you, that you can do far more for him and that he will be better off listing with you and your company. You can explain the many advantages to him of listing with a REALTOR, as follows:

Some Reasons Why the Homeowner Should List With a REALTOR

- The homeowner's ad attracts many kinds of people. Some phone in and set up an appointment. The homeowner remains at home all day waiting for the people to drive up. They never arrive. Perhaps they drove by, did not like the outside of the house and simply kept on driving. The homeowner does not know this and just waits, reluctant to leave in case they show up at a later hour.

- The homeowner's ad will attract speculators who are trying to "steal" a house, and other bargain hunters who have been looking for years. Some will be curious neighbors who had always wanted to see the way this type of house was decorated. All of these prospects are trying to save the same commission that the seller wants to save. They probably have experience at this, having bargained with other homeowners over a long period of time. In fact, they may have unlimited time to find a house.

- The homeowner on his own, lacks experience in selling real estate. Since it is not his business, his presentation is less effective. Although he may work hard, his chances of finding a ready buyer are limited. When a real estate company lists the house, a staff of active agents, working on a full time basis, are available. They are all familiar with the problems involved in selling a house. The sellers are free to go away on weekends or on extended vacations and simply leave a phone number where they can be reached should an offer to purchase be made.

- Prospective buyers don't always know precisely what they want or what value they can afford. They may want the house but not be acceptable for financing with a mortgage company. The real estate company agent screens all his prospects before leaving the office to show homes.

- There may be problems arranging financing. A large real estate company has many sources from which to obtain financing. They can shop around for the best terms.

- The real estate company knows the current market and can price the home realistically. The homeowner may read the ads that other homeowners have placed for similar homes, without being aware that they are overpriced and not being sold at these asking prices.

- Sellers and buyers find it difficult to negotiate a final sale. The real estate salesman is of great help in this area, since he acts as the go-between and the prospect tends to heed his advice.

- Prospective buyers ask questions that the seller cannot always answer: "Is your loan assumable? How much money do I need for closing?"

- Sellers are shy about asking questions of the prospects that they think are of a personal nature: "How much are you earning? How long have you been working? Is your wife presently employed? How much cash do you have? Do you have any current debts?"

- Prospective buyers may have objections that they do not feel comfortable bringing up with the sellers, but will not hesitate to mention to the agent. An experienced salesman knows how to handle these objections effectively.

Listen, Listen, Listen

It is important to find the reason for the sellers' move. Try to get the sellers in a conversational mood. Most people like to talk about themselves and their homes, are flattered by your interest and will react kindly towards you. You will be treated like an old friend. Ask questions to determine their urgency:

Are you happy about moving?
Are you going back home?
Have you found another home yet? How much cash will be required for its purchase?
When will your home be ready for occupancy?

Are they moving up? (better job, more money or prestige). Is this a case of separation or divorce? Are they moving because of financial difficulties? (loss of job, demotion, etc.). Is there illness in the family and is this the reason? The answers will soon give you a clear idea of their reasons, *if you listen.* Your attitude of sympathy and attention will continue to make them feel warmly toward you.

If the sellers are moving because of a better job and are possibly going where they have always wanted to live, be happy for them. By listening you will be able to determine their *urgency.* Then ask questions to determine their *selling experience:*

Have you owned any homes before this one?
Have you ever sold your own home?
Have you made any attempt to sell this one on your own?

Ask questions to determine the sellers' idea of value:

What improvements have you made?
What do you consider a fair price for your home?

Ask questions about neighborhood benefits, schools, churches, bus lines, shopping, etc. All these details are vital and should be ascertained at the time you list the property, in order not to jeopardize a future sale. (It is a good idea to inquire at this time if the seller is willing to hold a note or second trust, if required, and if so, for how much. Also ask if any of his selling costs are to be reimbursed by his employer.)

Do a minimum of talking. Ask questions and then listen to the sellers' needs. If you talk continuously, you miss vital information. Remember the saying: "When your jaw drops, your ears close." You should make favorable comments about the house, particularly if the family has made attractive improvements. Be sincere in your observations. Then listen to their comments.

Don't Overeducate the Homeowner

Do not tell the homeowner more than he can absorb. Even though the language of real estate selling is familiar to you, it may cause your seller to just nod his head in agreement, not really understanding what you are talking about. He may be confused and too ashamed to admit it. You should be able to sense this immediately.

A seller may call you in to "pick your brains" for information so that he can sell his home himself. If you tell him all you know on this first visit, you will have very little left about which to talk on your next. Real estate salesmen give more free information than do any other professionals. They do it in the name of "good will' and "future business." The doctor and lawyer charge a fee for advice and the man at the garage does his work and presents his bill. The plumber and the electrician even charge for their time getting to your home, before they even look to see what is wrong. Yet many real estate agents gladly and avidly give out free advice. Homeowners ask what you believe they can get for their homes if and when they will be ready to sell. They ask your advice about adding a room in the back instead of converting the garage into a family room. They ask your advice about refinancing. They even call you in, without any intention of listing their homes with you, to find out how much to ask when they put it on the market by themselves. Some may even ask you to help write the ad they will place. You do many of these things because you hope you will ultimately get the listing. Many, many times you work without knowing if you will ever get paid for this labor. An agent should not feel that, because he knows all about real estate, he must educate every person who asks a question about the subject. Some of his "pupils" might soon be taking the real estate exam and become his competitors. Be helpful and friendly but save some of your advice for the time after the homeowners have put their signatures on the listing agreement.

I learned to "hold back" the hard way. I was called in by friends who were being transferred and were planning to sell their home. I assumed that since they had called me, that they intended to give me the listing on their home. We spent a nice social evening. They were friendly and flattering, asking me all kinds of questions about selling homes. Then they thanked me profusely and confided that now they knew how and would try their hand at selling their home themselves.

There are dangers in dallying after you have the signed listing. Once as a rookie, after I had listed a house that a family had outgrown, I sat and chatted with the homeowners. I told them about investments and rental property. All very friendly. The next day the man came into the office, withdrew his listing and thanked me. He had decided that my advice was very sound. Since he did not need the proceeds of a sale of his home, he was going to put it up for rent. It seemed I had talked too much and had talked myself right out of the listing. I had, however, learned a valuable lesson. Know when to stop talking! When you have a signed listing agreement, say that you are anxious to get right back to the office to start working on it and *move fast*. I also have learned that the only time to discuss rentals and investments is when you are trying to get an investor to buy a rental property or make an investment.

Explaining Points

Some types of loans require "origination fees" which the seller must pay. These are usually expressed in terms of "points." (See *Points and Loan Fees* in Chapter Four.) A "point" is one percent of the loan amount. You should explain to the seller that if his house is sold under VA or FHA terms, he will probably have to pay these charges (except for one point which can be charged to the buyer). Points do fluctuate with money market conditions. Although they may be set at 3 when you list the property, they can go higher or lower by the time of settlement; the charges are made at that time. Some lenders will give a "firm commitment" (a guarantee on the number of points to be charged) when the loan application is taken. However, should VA or FHA interest rates change before settlement, the commitment is no longer effective, since it is based on the quoted interest rate remaining the same.

The Last Item On Your Agenda: "Setting the Price"

Sometimes, as I enter the house, Mr. Homeowner will ask me what I think his home will sell for. This is a hard question to answer at any time, since no one really can know what any house will eventually be sold for. My answer is that I will have a better idea after I have inspected his home. If he is insistent and keeps asking, I then tell him that I have to give it some thought. That I always try to get the highest possible price for any house that I list, but that it will only sell for whatever someone is willing to pay for it. Until I am sure that I have his listing, I avoid getting pinned down to a specific price. There are good reasons for this:

- The homeowner may have called me in simply to find out how much he can advertise his home for in the Sunday papers.
- The seller may already have selected the agent who will list his home (a friend or a relative) and is only looking for another opinion on price.
- The seller may actually be looking for a real estate agent and a

company to represent him, but has a definite price already fixed in his mind. At this time, if I have not yet gained his full confidence and trust and the price I quote is lower than the one he has in mind, he will rule me out immediately, even though he will politely allow me to waste my evening and think I am getting the listing.

- He may not be planning his move for five or six months. The value of his home will in all probability increase by then. He will only remember the price I quoted as of this date, and feel that I had quoted low because I wanted an "easy sale" or that this was probably the best my company could offer.

Try to price the home you are listing in a *realistic manner*. If the reason for selling is compelling enough, the seller should be induced to set his price in line with the going market for similar homes. A home priced right is a home easier to sell and faster to be sold. If it is listed too high, you will work harder getting other agents to show it and trying to sell it. Explain to the seller that even though his wood fence looks charming and cost him a great deal more than his neighbor's chain link fence, it will appraise for less because the appraiser figures that a chain link fence has a longer life than a fence of wood. Explain that the added room, or added appliances will influence the appraisal, but that he can expect little or nothing added to the appraised price where he "exchanged one wall for another" with either wood panel or wallpaper. However, the appearance is important and if the house shows well, prospective buyers will surely be influenced and consider it favorably and therefore be willing to pay more for it. It may become necessary to explain that although they have converted their garage into a family room and would like to add that cost to their asking price, they have actually "removed" the garage and should subtract the value of the garage. Explain to the sellers that "based on what homes similar to yours are selling for (show them the price range), I believe that your home should sell for between $40,000 and $45,000." Show them the highest and lowest prices that are on the listings you brought with you of current homes on the market or those recently sold. Point out the asking prices, appraisal values and selling prices.

It is true that every so often an over-priced house will sell at its asking price. This is rare, however, and you will generally find that when it did sell high, it had certain desirable features not found in the other similar properties. The house may have had exceptional decorating or been situated on a large park-like lot. The purchaser may have wanted this particular house and location because of a school district and was willing to pay a higher price to satisfy his need.

When the sellers tell you that their home is superior to all the other similar homes now on the market and that they must get more for theirs than you think it will bring, *don't reduce it to a battle, and don't argue!* Just agree as follows:

I appreciate how you feel—you want just as much as you can get for your home and so do we. However, if you set the price too high, you may be pricing yourself right out of the market. Prospective buyers look at more than one home when they are ready to buy and they do compare prices. I know you do not want a parade of people going through your home on their way to buying another one which is similar to yours in all ways except that the price is lower.

Show the sellers the price you suggest by writing it down. Then write down the selling costs and what they may expect to net, etc., so that they cannot later claim that you quoted them a larger amount. If the sellers still insist that you list their home at a higher figure than you feel it should have, you may still possibly get it sold at that figure, but it will take longer and you will have to work harder to do so. Tell the sellers that you will set *their price* on the listing, but that you will be "testing the market" for the next two weeks at which time you will return to talk it over with them. After a week or two, if there has been little or no action, return bringing with you copies of newspaper ads showing what advertising your office has done. If the house was shown by other agents, have their comments and reactions. Report on your own progress. If similar homes have been sold during this period, get their asking prices and selling prices, and have all this information with you.

Selecting the Best Method of Financing for Your Client, the Seller

Calculate what your client will net (i.e., the cash amount to be returned to him after all his selling costs) for each possible method of financing, and show him how you calculate this. Then explain why you suggest the financing method or methods you do choose. It may not be the method that will net him the most, but it will assure a more rapid sale where needed. For example, although an assumption sale may yield your client the best return (no points to be paid), you are aware that the cash down payment required is too high to attract many buyers. Therefore, you may want to recommend FHA or VA financing requiring a low down payment on the part of the purchaser, even though the seller nets less. I attempt to list my clients' houses so that they will be attractive to more than one class of purchasers and therefore get sold faster. It is important that the seller understands what you are recommending and why. You do not want a surprised client at settlement because he didn't realize that points would be charged to him.

Should you get in a jam because of rapid changes in the financing market, ask your broker for help. I recall one case which almost gave me ulcers. My client had agreed to pay points on a VA sale of his home; points were 4 at the time the contract was signed and the mortgage money market was easing up. In fact it eased up so much that by the time of closing a few months later, the VA interest rate had dropped, but points had jumped to 7. Even though I had warned my client that points on a VA loan could not be determined until the actual day of settlement, he refused to settle and pay this rate. In desperation I went to my sales manager. He worked out a special deal with one of the finance companies to charge only 5 points on this case. My client was satisfied and I breathed a sigh of relief. Finance companies are usually competing for the business of real estate companies. You will sometimes find the one you use frequently anxious to do your broker a favor to save a sale. Of course a salesman cannot depend upon this solution, but it is there if you are really in trouble on financing.

■ **GETTING THE SIGNATURE ON THE LISTING AGREEMENT**

After you have gained the homeowners' attention and interest with your enthusiasm and know-how, you need to nail down the listing with signatures on the listing form. To keep their interest, walk through the home, making notations about what you see and ask what goes with the home. Use a tape measure and pace off the rooms (even though you are familiar with the size of every room in this particular type of home). You do want to impress them with your professionalism. Ask what is to be negotiated with the sale (freezer, drapes, TV antenna, personal property, etc.). Lead the way and make for the kitchen. This should be your last stop. Suggest that you all sit down "here where it's comfortable and cozy and where I can write it all down—I don't want to miss any of it." Then sit and write. They will follow your lead and sit. Continue by saying: "You have a lovely home. I imagine you will hate to leave it after doing so much work on it and fixing it up so attractively."

Start filling in the listing form, transferring your notes to the form. Ask to see the house plat for the lot and block numbers. Don't guess at the size of the lot but get the exact area in square feet. Ask who holds the loan mortgage and determine the interest rate, monthly payments, etc. Get the account number and amount of taxes. Find out if there is more than one mortgage on the property. Let them tell you the things that come to mind. Ask about items you noticed as you had walked through the rooms, if they neglect to mention them: "I noticed that you have a humidifier." Then write it down. If you have not seen a dishwasher, comment on this: "You don't have a dishwasher." They will know that you have examined their home thoroughly. Point out one or more of the attractive features of their home and comment on how great it will look in "the ad we will place in the paper." *Always assume that you will be getting the listing.*

Never Knock Another Agent or His Company

The seller may mention that another agent has told him he can get $5,000 more than the going price for his home, or some other such nonsense. Just disregard this and say nothing. This "agent" may just happen to be a relative or his best friend or the father of their baby sitter, or someone to whom the listing has already been promised, and you are being tested. Do not disparage the other agent or his company.

Never Accept a Drink That Is Stronger Than Strong Tea!

If, while you are relaxing with the sellers, they offer you a drink, make sure it is nothing stronger than water, tea, coffee or a soft drink. An agent I know went out to list a house unaware that the husband and wife were on the verge of a separation because of the husband's drinking problem. The agent was offered a beer by the man, and accepted. Both husband and wife signed the listing agreement. Later the wife changed her mind and tried to withdraw from the listing. She claimed that the agent had been responsible for getting the husband drunk and forcing him to sign while "under the influence."

Perseverance

While on floor duty one day, I received a phone call from a woman who said she wasn't sure whether she wanted to list her property for sale or for rent; that she would be moving soon. Since I was then a rookie, I asked my sales manager to go along with me to help convince the homeowners that they would be better off selling their home rather than renting it to others, since they would be moving from the state. I set up an appointment for that evening.

The family had been out grocery shopping and, when we arrived at their home, were just unloading their car. My sales manager sat down at the kitchen table, cleared the space in front of him and immediately relaxed them with friendly chit-chat. The woman left her meat defrosting on the kitchen sink and sat down with us so that she too would hear everything he had to say. I let him do all the talking since he was the "pro" and I observed him closely. (He was a big, jolly man, with an easy relaxed manner and seemed to be quite comfortable in the small kitchen chair.)

He explained that one advantage of selling rather than renting was that they would have the money to buy another home in their new location. They had not, however, considered making any final decision this day and now refused to commit themselves. My sales manager tried to close them many times but they remained negative. He just smiled and tried another approach. The woman got up and sat down several times. My sales manager never budged from that chair! He just sat, smiled, nodded his head and was very friendly. *He just assumed that he would get the listing.* She kept looking at the sink where the meat was defrosting into its own little pool. My sales manager never even seemed to notice this. They were, however, too polite to invite us to leave. (P.S. We got the listing that night.)

While driving back to the office, I asked my sales manager how long he had planned to stay glued to that chair, since the homeowners had been squirming for an hour, watching their meat defrost into the sink. "Till I got the listing, of course," was his reply.

Trial Closes to Get the Signature on the Listing

After you have entered all the items about the house on the listing form and before you ask for the signature, if you are not quite sure in your mind that you actually have their consent to the listing, try some trial listing closes:

- Can I order a VA appraisal for you at this time? It will make it easier for you if I order it now, saving the time involved for the appraisal to be made and the results obtained should we get an immediate offer. If I order it for you now, I can follow up on the appraiser's progress, and if you are not home when he calls

I can go to your home with him, so that he will not delay making the appraisal. An appraiser gives very short notice when he calls to appraise.

- I have a prospective buyer who has been looking for a home such as yours. I have been working with him for weeks now. I told him I would call him just as soon as one came on the market. May I show him your home? (You should, of course, have an actual prospect for this type of home.)

Never Be Afraid to Ask for the Listing

Many agents are afraid to ask for the listing and as a result never get it. If you are sure that it is not already listed with another agent, *ask for it*. The homeowners can either say they will not list their home with you, or they can say yes.

A Salesman May Be Called Upon to Play Many Roles

If a family is on the verge of separation, you act as mediator and hope that they continue to remain friendly long enough to sign the listing form. One day I received the following phone call: "Can you please come right over to list my house for sale? Bring a 'For Sale' sign with you." I hastily gathered together a folder containing listing form, comparables and copies of listings of similar, sold and appraised homes. Putting the sign in my car, I took off. I found a very sad young man pacing the floor of a neat, modern and well-furnished house. He told me that he had been married for six months and separated for four. That he had purchased the house before marrying and never had a chance to transfer his wife's name onto the deed. He was not living in the house, having moved out to allow her to remain. He kept hoping for a reconciliation. "Could you put the 'For Sale' sign on the front lawn without actually putting the house on the market?" he pleaded. "I think that when she comes home and sees I am serious about selling and that she will have to move, she will make up her mind about us getting together." He further explained that he was taking her to dinner that evening and the sign might do the trick. I put the sign on his lawn, told him I would wait for the next morning to put the house on the market, meanwhile explaining in the office that it could not be shown until the next day. Bright and early I phoned him. They had reconciled and were happily sharing the same nest.

Sometimes an agent must arrange to have his listed house cleaned or painted and repaired, because the sellers or a tenant have left it in poor condition and the purchasers, after their pre-inspection of the property, are refusing to accept it and the sellers have already moved away. Other times the keys don't fit or a pipe has burst. The lawn may need cutting. The agent may have to arrange to have the utilities transferred for an out-of-town purchaser or seller. You never know what conditions are sometimes written into contracts and accepted by sellers; I have seen agents going to a settlement with a towel bar or a toilet seat, because the contract specified that these be replaced!

The Guaranteed Sale

Many real estate companies will guarantee the sale of his home to a homeowner who cannot purchase another one elsewhere while his current home remains unsold. Generally, the real estate company considers a number of things: Is the home well-located? Is it priced right? Has an appraisal been ordered? Is there a demand for this type of home? The guarantee generally specifies that if the house is not sold by the company within a stated period of time, the real estate company will buy the house at an agreed upon price. The company will then keep the house in "inventory" and attempt to resell it or rent it.

Most REALTORS guarantee sales from time to time. Where the owner will soon be moving from the state and does not want to chance the home remaining unsold, your broker might be willing to guarantee the sale, if the price is right. The listing will then provide that your company has a limited time (i.e., 90 days) to sell the property at the asking price, after which time the company will buy it at a determined price (a percentage below the asking price, to cover commissions and expenses).

There is another type of guaranteed sale that some homeowners are given when being transferred out of the area by their employer. The employing company, usually through a real estate subsidiary (e.g., Homequity), will guarantee the employee a fixed dollar amount for his home, after appraising it. However, the homeowner has the option of getting more than this guaranteed amount by selling the house himself or through a real estate company, for a higher price, within a specified time period. By all means, you should take such a listing if you can get it. The wording on the listing must reflect the guarantee given by the company and sometimes the company will supply the wording. Should the homeowner's company actually buy the house, it is immediately put on the market by the company, through one of the local real estate companies. If your real estate company is selected, you are considered the listing agent if you originally had the listing with the employee that moved.

■ NOW THAT YOU HAVE THE SIGNED LISTING

There are many things that can be done to help sell the house you have just listed, satisfactorily and FAST. SHOWMANSHIP SELLS. The house should project warmth and welcome to the prospective buyers who enter. Here are *some tested techniques* which, with little effort on the part of the sellers, can accomplish a quicker sale at a better price, by making the home show to its best advantage. You should suggest them to the seller tactfully.

Suggestions to the Sellers

First impressions are most important. When a prospect approaches the house that has a scraggly lawn, unpainted fence and exterior and drooping gutters, he will start thinking negatively about the house before he has even walked in the door. The lawn should be kept trimmed and edged; the walk clear of debris and the flower beds neat and trim. In the winter time, the snow and ice should be removed from any walks leading to the house. Any paint touchups to improve the property, especially around doors, windows and gutters should be done before the house is shown to prospective buyers. Any loose shingles and tiles should be replaced. Many buyers will not consider any home in need of repair and they are unable to imagine how the house with faded walls and unkempt condition, can be made to look after it is spruced up.

Have the seller "put himself in the buyer's shoes" and pretend he is walking into his own home for the first time as a prospective buyer. Then have him make out a list of all the things that he would like to have done if he were considering its purchase. Then he should attempt to do them.

There is nothing as depressing as coming in from the bright sunshine into a gloomy, poorly-lit kitchen. The kitchen is the heart of the home and should be well-lit and spotless. A cheerful kitchen says *welcome*. It should be kept uncluttered with no dirty dishes in the sink. Women purchasers are also sensitive about bathrooms, so they should be clean and orderly. Adding some greenery in the entry hall and flowers on the kitchen and living room tables; having the hi-fi playing softly in the background; a glowing fire in the den or living room fireplace; the aroma of freshly baked bread, all brighten a chilly day and have sold many a home.

A gurgling toilet and a dripping faucet with discolored sink quickly call attention to possible faulty plumbing. Any loose door knobs? Creaking floors? Loose railings? Now is the time to fix them. Paint any dingy or badly marked walls. Keep all surfaces clear for an uncluttered look and therefore a more spacious appearance. Pack away any unnecessary articles which will not be needed. The seller will have to pack them anyway when he moves. The room size will "grow" without the clutter. The closets should be rearranged to make them appear larger. If the seller has told you that he will be selling certain items of furniture before moving, have him do so now, especially if they will detract from the overall appearance when the house is being shown. The house should be kept as quiet as possible, without too many people present when it is being shown.

I once made an appointment to show a house whose sole residents were a man, his wife and a teen-aged son. However, when I arrived with my prospects, we could hear the music clearly down the street. The parents had gone out for the day, and the son had fifteen assorted friends lounging on all the chairs and three visiting dogs galloping through the rooms. The hi-fi was blasting away and everyone was talking loudly at the same time. In order to inspect the rooms, we kept tripping over outstretched legs. One of the dogs, a great dane, decided to inspect with us and kept sniffing at our legs. Since the woman prospect was scared of anything on four legs, she kept hiding behind her husband. We all felt like intruders at someone's party and couldn't wait to get out. I ran interference for them and we finally made it to the car. The sad part of this was that the sellers were extremely anxious to get the house sold and my prospects were right for this type of house, except it never had a chance.

If the sellers have a cat or dog that they plan to either give away or board, have them do it before the house is to be shown. (You can't give your teen-aged children away, however, but they should be made to understand the rules.) Suggest that the sellers remain in the background while the home is being shown, and volunteer no information. This is most important because it can kill a sale.

I had a very good prospect for a home who loved the location and the appearance. The seller, however, bragged about the fact that a new motor had just been installed in the dishwasher. I saw the prospect quickly turn to the refrigerator, wondering when that motor would go and need to be replaced. Once outside, he told me that he had second thoughts about buying this home and that perhaps he wanted a newer one after all—one with new appliances. The house we had just left was three years old!

Stress to the woman who is selling her home that if she is thinking of negotiating the sale of her freezer, drapes, etc., with the buyer of her home, she must wait until there is in fact a bona fide signed contract before trying to do so. It can only divert the prospect who is inspecting her home from the important considerations in making his purchase. My prospects and I arrived to inspect a home one day, only to have the seller call the woman aside as we walked in. She attempted to sell her the freezer which was not included in the listing. The prospect was so busy considering this freezer, that she never did see the house.

Discourage the seller from discussing price, terms or possession, with any prospects inspecting his home. Have him refer them back to the salesman who is better equipped to bring such negotiations to a favorable conclusion.

The seller should never apologize to the prospect for the appearance of his home. The prospect knows that it is being lived in. Neither should he feel that he has to socialize with the prospect. A showing appointment is not a social call. The seller can welcome the agent and his people at the door but then he should remain in the background. The seller must let the salesman do the selling. He should not tag along while the salesman shows the house to the prospect. Explain that if you need his assistance, you will find him. Also explain that each agent has his own style of selling. Sometimes the seller feels that the agent is not showing enough of the house or perhaps not pointing out each and every item. Explain to the seller that the agent may be watching his prospect for a specific reaction.

A frantic seller phoned the office one day to complain that I had practically run through his home, and was in such a hurry that I never even showed my prospect how he had carpeted and shelved the hall closet. Actually his call interrupted the contract I was busy writing on his home. The people loved it as soon as they saw it. This house was just what they were looking for. They couldn't wait to get back to the office so that I could explain the financing and write up the offer.

If you properly prepare the sellers for the showing process, they will understand that most of the selling is actually done on the ride to the home, and completed on the ride back to the office. If an agent goes through the home rather fast, he may have a reason for doing so. Either his prospects are not at all interested and have told him so, or they cannot wait to write the offer.

The Key to It All

Sometimes, after you have listed a house, the seller is hesitant about giving up a key. The woman may have antiques or valuable knickknacks spread around on shelves or tables. Explain the importance of availability of the home for showing during the day. Many hurried, bona fide prospects, who are very well qualified to buy, have trains or planes to catch and are on limited time. Suggest that the family pack these treasures away. They will need to do this sooner or later for their move. Perhaps the family hesitates giving up the key because there is a dog on the premises. Mark the key and the listing with a note giving the dog's name, whether he is friendly, barks, etc., and where he will be kept during the day when the family is not at home. You will need the key for the appraiser, termite inspector, etc., even after the showings.

Other Advice for the Sellers

Explain that you will be putting a 'For Sale' sign on the property and that the agents from your company and from other cooperating companies, will be inspecting and showing their home. *I always advise the sellers that, even though I am listing their home, I may not necessarily be the one who actually sells it.* Their home may be in the colonial style, and all my prospects for the next few weeks may be ranch or Cape Cod style buyers. I do, however, add that *I will be the one who sees that it gets promoted, advertised, shown and sold.* I will put it into our multiple listing service as soon as I get back to the office and will give it maximum coverage, seeing that all of our agents know about it and inspect it. I further advise them that I represent them and will keep them informed; that I am always available to answer any questions that they may have; that should a contract offer come into the office, no matter who writes it, I or my sales manager will be out to present it to them and fully explain it.

Make sure the sellers understand the many things you have told them. Then further explain:

- The company's advertising policy.
- The advantages of the MLS service (if your company has this service, or any other co-op setup that your office does use).
- All about VA and FHA financing.
- How you will be contacting them as soon as any contract offers are written in order to present these offers to them.

If you are ordering an appraisal, be sure to pick up a copy of the plat of the house and a check for the appraisal fee. Show the sellers, on paper, approximately how much they may expect to net from the sale, depending upon which way the house is sold. Give the sellers a copy of the listing agreement they have just signed, explain that you are available at all times (and keep yourself available); pick up the key (try it to make sure it fits!) and give them your personal card, together with a Home-owner's Showing Card for other agents to sign when showing or inspect-ing the home; thank them and leave. Remember, don't stay and linger after you have the signed listing! Before you drive off, make sure that your "For Sale" sign has been hammered into the lawn, with your name prominently displayed. Take a picture of the house with your sign on the property. You can show this picture to prospective purchasers and possibly influence them, if the house shows well.

■ MEANWHILE, BACK AT THE OFFICE

After you have the signed listing agreement, head back to the office and start working. The sooner you get the listing into your company "flip" files and into the multiple listing service (if you have one), the sooner other agents will start showing the home and possibly bring in an offer. Some selfish agents will keep a listing from other agents in the company hoping to sell it themselves (pocket listing). This is un-ethical because the agent is not properly representing his client. His client is not getting the advantages of many agents working for him towards the sale of his home.

Start a folder. Make copies of the plat, listing, etc. Fill out the necessary forms in order to put it into the office records and co-op sys-tem. Tag and number the key. If your office has a lock box system (a locked metal box which is secured on the front door or knob, and per-mits all agents with a master key to obtain the house key which is contained in the box), arrange for this. If there is an appraisal to be ordered, start the ball rolling. Remember, an appraiser's ability to gain easy access to the property is very important. If the appraiser cannot get into the house, it could mean a delay in getting the house appraised. Advise whether or not the owner is home during the day and, if both work, provide the real estate office phone number and your own name and number on the appraisal request.

Make an entry into your diary for follow-up in about ten days, so that you can call the sellers and advise them of your progress, and pos-sibly get the price reduced, if it was set too high. Make one other entry to remind you of the expiration date of the listing and resolve to get the house sold before that date. Then get up on your "soap box" and ·announce to all that you have just listed this house and it is terrific.

Start An Entry System on the Folder

It is an excellent idea to make important notations directly on the file folder. This has saved me much time in a busy day. After I have the initial paper work done on a new listing, I start making my entries right on the front of the folder. The first entry is the name of my client, his wife's name, the home and office phone number. It will not be necessary for me to dig through the entire file whenever I want to call them. I note the MLS number in a corner and under this I enter if there are any service contracts on the house (heating, air conditioning, water heater) and if there is a swimming pool membership or other such pertinent considerations. Should I be ordering a VA or FHA appraisal, I write the date on the folder and when I think the appraiser is due. (If an appraisal has been ordered, I enter this fact instead.) When the appraiser later calls in to set up an appointment to appraise the property, I enter the appointment date on the folder and in my diary. Whenever the sellers advise me they will be away for any length of time, I get the phone numbers where they can be reached in case a contract offer is brought in. Any closing information will be added as I am informed of it (moving dates, etc.) and the last item will be the scheduled time of settlement. I have seen agents go away on vacation or just be away for a few hours, and have emergencies come up on their cases. If I cannot be reached, my sales manager or another agent, can pick up any one of my file folders and all the pertinent information and phone numbers are visible on the front cover.

The Importance of Good Advertising

Advertising is just "telling the truth" attractively. Read some of the ads put out by successful real estate companies to prove this. To sell homes and attract purchasers, you don't need an elaborate office. All you need to do is run good ads and list your phone number, and people will respond. The important thing is to get the prospects to come out—they will if an ad catches their attention and intrigues them. I have seen this work many times. On the other hand, if the home being advertised is an extremely attractive one, but the ad is worded in such a way that it seems ordinary, the phones won't even ring.

Write the Ad Yourself

The right ad should attract qualified prospects. Before you write it, be sure you know your audience and direct the ad to them. After you have gathered together all the facts about the property, decide the kind of family it would attract (a large one or a small one, etc.) and write an eye-catching headline. You want to attract the prospects' attention and interest right at the beginning. You can advertise a "teeny weenie" house on a barren lot as "cozy home with unobstructed view." If there is no road leading to the house, you say: "Secluded home. Get away from the hustle and bustle." (I once went to inspect a house that had been advertised as having a stream on the property, only to find that the stream was in the basement.)

Give a lot of thought to the ad you write and concentrate on proclaiming value. A true bargain produces qualified callers. List the features that should appeal to the type of people you are trying to reach. Use your imagination and appeal to their emotions, by offering something you think they are looking for. Make it exciting but make sure it is accurate. You are selling more than a shelter. You are *selling a home*. A well-written ad should also attract other agents who may have prospects looking for the type of home you are trying to sell. They will call your office for a co-op if the ad describes what they are searching for. The more people showing the home, the better your chances of a favorable sale.

Those Company "For Sale" Signs Really Work

I once got a call from a woman who, fortunately, had a sense of humor. She had just walked out of her house and saw my sign on her property, boldly advertising her home for sale. She called to tell me that this was the first she knew that she was selling her home! (I had listed the property next door and had no available sign with me, so my son was helping out, and you know what happened.) In another instance, one of our agents leaned a sign he had just taken out of his garage against the side of his house and went back inside to answer his phone. He came out to find a couple inspecting his property.

Calls that result from a company sign on a listed property are generally from prospects who have driven by, liked what they have seen on the outside and are genuinely interested in the house. Sometimes a neighbor may have a friend "who was waiting for this kind of house to be put up for sale." An agent driving his prospect to inspect other properties may have the house sign pointed out to him by his prospect, who may ask to see the house. A renter, walking his dog, may see the sign and be interested enough to call for information (and hopefully ask for the agent whose name is on the sign—*yours*).

"Like the ad said—house with a view!"

After the house is sold, don't forget to put the SOLD sign on the property. This, again, is good advertising for you and for your company. Now all of those neighbors and potential sellers of homes who have been watching and wondering, can see what a great job you and your company have done in selling this house and know for whom to ask. So be sure your sign is up as soon as you list a house. If you have someone else do it for you, check to be sure it has been done and is clearly visible. I have always found my signs to be a great source for leads.

Checking In With Your Client, the Sellers

Good service depends on good communications. Call the sellers to advise them on your progress before they start worrying and call you. If, after a few weeks, the home you listed is not sold although it has been shown continually, or it is not being shown by other agents because of price, etc., call the sellers for an appointment to go over and discuss with them what else you can do about getting their home sold. Have with you copies of any advertising your company has run since the listing was brought in. Also, any comments from other agents who have inspected and shown the home. Explain to the sellers that there are *three basic reasons why a house does not sell:*

1 ▪ *Location.* A house may be on a hill, in a valley or have a sloping back yard with poor drainage. It may be badly located and far from shopping, schools, etc. It may be placed poorly on the lot or back up to a garage or over-lit shopping center.

2 ▪ *Condition.* A house may be in bad need of repairs and completely run down, and many prospective purchasers are automatically turned off, so the house remains unsold.

3 ▪ *Price.* A house may be overpriced, and prospective purchasers pass it by for more realistically priced homes.

If the sellers' home does not fall into the first two categories (location and condition) you know that the culprit has to be PRICE. Since we know that sellers find it hard to separate sentiment and emotional price from the realistic price, they have to be brought down to earth. No one pays for the sellers' sentimental value.

Talk to the sellers. They may have a change of heart about the price they had originally insisted they had to get. Possibly, since the house was listed, their conditions have changed and they have now found the home they were seeking to buy. Perhaps they now realize that people are not "standing in line" to buy their home. Before you walk through the door, they may be asking you if they could perhaps lower the price in order to get it sold faster. Always carry a "change of status" form with you. You will need both signatures on this form, in order to change the asking price.

chapter three

PROSPECTING
FOR CLIENTS

▪ HOW THE PROS
DO IT

The successful, money making real estate salesman does not wait for prospects to come to him. He actively seeks them out no matter where he goes. The following are some suggestions on how to get prospects:

- Read your local newspapers. Look for newcomers coming into town as they will need housing, especially if they are being hired locally.
- Get friendly with the people at local motels, hotels and restaurants. Leave cards with them.
- Cultivate the people to whom you have sold homes and with whom you have done business. Call on them. Remember, a satisfied buyer or seller is a source of referrals.
- Use a follow-up system for correspondence and contacts. Remember to send birthday cards to people you know and also to those in the hospital, etc.
- Mix with people. Don't sit around the office and wait. Call on people. The more calls you make, the more sales you will have.

Be A Joiner

Join every organization for which you have the time and meet all the members you can. Each one you meet has some real estate information that can be useful to you. If he is not presently in the market to buy or sell, he may know someone who is. In addition, at some later date he may decide to buy or sell a house and remember you. Dare to be a little different and dynamic in your manner, so that you stand out from the crowd. Be friendly but look and act successful. Have humility and don't brag about how much you know. Let others discover for themselves. When you are asked for your opinion on the current housing market or on investments in real estate, or housing in general, always try to be optimistic and enthusiastic about the future. Have confidence in your own ability, so that people will want to deal with you and refer all their friends and relatives to you, knowing you will be helpful and that you are knowledgeable.

Always remember that *nobody likes a loser.* If people think you are making money, they will feel that you must be a very good salesman and doing all the right things. Be imaginative, have empathy and above all, *give out your cards!*

Talk Real Estate

You would be surprised to find how many people will surround you at a party or at a gathering of ·a few friends, once they learn that you are in real estate. When they find out that you are also successful, making lots of money and investing on your own, they will be even more interested in what you have to say. You won't have to announce that you are in real estate. It will get around. Many of the questions will be the kind that you cannot answer, such as: "How much do you think my house is worth?" Those asking this generally aren't even thinking of selling. They simply want the reassurance that their homes have increased in value. You can always say that it has probably appreciated in value, because all real estate appreciates in value over a period of time. Be friendly. You never know when they may decide to move to your area and look you up, or they may send friends out to see you— friends looking for a home to buy.

Keep In Touch With Them All

Your satisfied customers may have convinced some of their friends that this was a great area in which to settle and you were a great agent to find that home for them. These happy homeowners become part of your circle of referrals. You must remember to keep in touch with them at least every six months. Perhaps a satisfied homeowner who purchased his home with your helpful assistance, has already been notified that he is being transferred out of the area, or is now thinking of a larger or smaller home and getting ready to look for such a home. *Keep in touch with them all.* Send out cards on Thanksgiving and calendars at Christmas time. Phone them as they may have mislaid the card you gave them so long ago.

WHO DO YOU KNOW?

From school or college?
From your church?
From your old job?
From your old neighborhood?
From your lodge or club?
From your civic activities?
Through your wife, family and children?
Because of your favorite sports or hobbies?
Who sells you your fishing tackle?
Who owns your bowling alley?
Who are your best luncheon club friends?
Who plays bridge with you?
Who is your best friend?
Who was your best man?
Who was the groom at the last wedding you attended?
Who heads your local Parent Teacher's Association?
Who is the principal of your local high school?
Who is your son's or daughter's scoutmaster?
Who gives your children music lessons?
Who lives next door to you?
Who heads your local Veteran's Organization?
Who heads your local Lions Club, Kiwanis, etc.?
Who heads your bank?
Who manages your local theatre?
Who manages or owns your local five and dime store?
Who runs your local delicatessen?
Who owns your hardware store?
Who sells you meat? Groceries?
Who cuts your hair? Your wife's and children's?
Who soles your shoes?
Who sells you tobacco?
Who serves you lunch?
Who sold you your dog?
Who is your veterinarian?
Who sold you your automobile?
Who sells you gas, tires, lubrication?
Who is your nearest used car dealer?

Who sold you your furniture? Your refrigerator and stove?
Who sold you your radio, piano, television? Who repairs them?
Who services or sells oil burners?
Who made your awnings, storm windows, screens?
Who insulated your house?
Who sold you your lightning rods?
Who sold you your fence?
Who owns the lumber yard?
Who is your painter? Decorator?
Who waxes your floors? Stores your rugs?
Who sells you coal or oil?
Who does your plumbing? Electrical work?
Who screened your porch?
Who upholstered your furniture?
Who sells you suits, hats, shoes?
Who sold your wife her fur coat?
Who sells your wife dresses, hats, shoes?
Who sells you office supplies? Who prints your stationery?
Who sells you Christmas cards?
Who sells you insurance?
Who does your income tax?
Who is your lawyer?
Who is your doctor? Dentist? Druggist? Nurse?
Who sold your family their eyeglasses?
Who sells you jewelry? Fixes your watch?
Who made your latest family photograph?
Who does your dry cleaning? Your laundry?
Who is your local chief of police?
Who is chief of your local fire department?
Who is your Justice of the Peace?
Who is your postmaster or letter carrier?
Who is on your local election board?
Who is your florist?
Who is your family undertaker?
Who recently received a salary increase?
Who has a son or daughter about to be married?
Who is getting a job transfer?

The Tenant As A Prospect

If a family is looking for a home to rent and is qualified to buy a home, think of them as "possible purchasers" instead of just "renters" while showing them homes. Some people can well afford to buy but have not considered it and no one has thought to approach them on it.

One of my rental listings was once advertised in the newspapers. A man and his wife who had just arrived from another state came into the office in response to this ad. I convinced them it would be to their advantage to make an offer to purchase this rental home and then took their offer to the owner of the property. He was delighted with the idea of selling the property instead of renting it and quickly accepted the contract offer.

I have also found an excellent source of prospective buyers right in the homes being shown for sale. They are the *tenants already living there.* These tenants may never have considered buying a home since no one has approached them with this suggestion. If you can show the renter the advantages and benefits of home ownership (such as tax benefits and equity appreciation) over renting, you may ring up another sale. I have written a contract offer on the kitchen table while the tenant was doing her laundry, had her and her husband sign it, driven to the landlords' home to present the offer and get it signed, and then driven back to the purchasers with the signed contract. If the home currently occupied by tenants is inadequate for their needs, I find this out while inspecting the property and then try to find one that is right for the family. If they cannot afford to buy now, I can at least try to find them a home to rent and earn a rental commission and good will for the future.

The "Open House" As A Source Of Prospects

Before becoming a real estate salesman, I thought that "having an open house" meant that someone was giving a party with all doors open wide and everyone welcome, and deposit your gift on the table near the door as you come in. Actually, holding open house means that you are advertising that a house currently on the market for sale, will be held open and available to other agents and homeseekers on a particular day and during a specified period (generally 1 P.M. to 5 P.M.). One or two agents will be in the house to welcome any prospects and agents who show up and they do not need to phone for an appointment before coming out during open house. Try to make the ad as attractive as possible, and detail the directions to the house. Sunday is a good day, since you want both husband and wife to come out. You put up some signs along the route described in the ad, making it easy to find the advertised house.

"Open houses" are effective because many people who are thinking of buying a home, are reluctant to go to a real estate company. Perhaps they are not quite sure what they are looking for and fear they will be obligated to the company or agent who will show them homes. Some feel they may be pestered with phone calls or high pressured into buying and would rather screen out the houses on their own. They know that if they come out and inspect an open house, they can leave whenever they choose. They do not know that at each open house sit highly qualified real estate salesmen, who welcome them at the door with a broad smile and a handshake, gently lead them around the house, and then perhaps back to the kitchen table for a trial close.

There are some people who spend each and every weekend, weather permitting, driving around inspecting models and open houses. Sometimes they do find a home that they like and buy. However, you will soon recognize those who make a hobby of inspecting homes but have no intention of buying—if you sit at open houses you will run into them often. They will not buy because if they do, they will then have no place to go on future Sundays.

When holding open house, it is a good idea to have a second agent with you. Some prospects may be interested in buying a home, but they may want a different style of home or one in a different price range. If you know of another listing closeby that will fit their needs, one agent can drive the family to inspect that house while the second agent attends to the open house.

Always greet the prospects at the door with a broad smile and a hearty welcome. Have them *sign in when they first enter* and get their phone numbers. It is difficult to get it after they have walked through the house, if they are not interested in this particular house. If you get their name and phone number and then find what they are looking for, you can follow up this lead. On the kitchen table, have contracts, copies of the listing and the plat of the property. Also, for your own personal use, have a list of other homes being held open plus other similar listings currently on the market, so that if the prospects have the time and want to look further, you or your partner can drive them to one of the other listed homes.

I once held "Open House" with another agent at a small ranch style home. A young couple barely glanced around as they walked through. They did, however, say that this was not really what they had in mind—they wanted a more modern house. I was able to set up an appointment with them for the next morning to see this "terrific house that is just what you are looking for." I sold them this house the next day and listed theirs. We put a "For Sale" sign on their home. That same night, their next door neighbor called us. She had a cousin who had been looking for such a house to come on the market. We gladly sold it to her. Sometimes you get "lucky," but only if you know how to take advantage of every opportunity.

Long Distance Referrals

Your REALTOR may have a co-op arrangement with brokers in other areas of the country; find out about it. Many times, when I am called to list a house, the sellers will tell me where they are planning to move and may ask if I know of a reliable broker in that state. Through our co-op referral service I can supply them with a name of an associated broker. Furthermore, I will sometimes call on their behalf and arrange an appointment. One day, a woman to whom I had previously sold a home, phoned saying her brother was moving to another state. Could I possibly arrange to have him met at the airport there and help him find a home? I took down all the information she could furnish about price and room size, etc., and relayed this information to a co-operating broker. Her brother was met the next day at the airport and was delighted with the homes he was shown. I was pleasantly surprised when the commission was added to my paycheck for this referral, since he had purchased one of the homes shown.

▪ MANAGE YOUR TIME EFFICIENTLY

You can squander your time gossiping with your co-workers in the office, socializing on the phone and taking long lunch hours, or you can fill the hours creatively. It is reflected in your commission check. Manage your time efficiently. Use it to create new business and re-activate old prospects; familiarize yourself with the area you will be working and where the current listings are; inspect homes currently on the market, and compare the prices. Organize your work. Do things in the order of their importance. It will conserve your time and the salesman's time is money.

Keep A Diary and A Notebook

Get a diary and use it. Your first entries should be your floor duty times. After that, the appointment dates for showing homes to prospects and the times of scheduled settlements on homes should be recorded. Work all other appointments such as listing and inspection of properties around these times. The remainder of the time is where you work in your personal appointments and chores (dentist, shopping, etc.). A reminder: *Don't forget to consult your diary each day!*

Don't get carried away with paperwork. One girl in our office developed her own elaborate system. She made duplicate files on every case that she had in process. In the beginning it was simple enough. She carried a few files wherever she went. Soon she needed a briefcase to contain her files. Now, after four years, she walks in each day looking like a busy bell-hop, with two briefcases under each arm. Agents have different ways to keep control of their leads, prospects and possible sources of referrals. Some make notations and their coat pockets bulge with small pieces of paper containing penciled reminders. Some agents carry around an elaborate card file system; others have developed their own personalized systems.

A few years ago, I devised a method that has worked very well for me. In addition to my diary, I carry a small spiral notebook. I make all my notations in this book. It can be opened flat and the pages easily torn out when I have attended to the items noted on the pages. This book replaces the many scraps of paper that I had been stuffing into pocket and purse, which were so easily lost. Instead of having to ask my associates: "Has anyone seen a small slip of paper with a name and phone number on it?" I just open this little book and read my notations. I date the top of each page. My notations can be made any time and any place. While driving, if I think of something needing attention, I jot it down when I stop for the next traffic light. When I return to the office, I glance through the new items, take care of those needing immediate attention and cross them from the page. The items needing transfer to my diary are so entered.

Your Working Tools

Just about every day in the office, an agent will ask to borrow a pen. I would hate to lose a sale because I didn't have the pen needed for a prospective buyer to sign an offer to purchase. I carry at least three pens at all times. You never can tell; two may run dry. Be prepared. Always have available:

- Listing forms (for rental and sale).
- Contract forms (purchase offers, deposit receipts, etc.).

- Lease forms and credit applications.
- Promissory notes (in case the purchaser is new in the area and has not as yet opened a checking account).
- Mortgage financing guide book.
- Two pads of paper (one for you to figure costs and one for the prospect to doodle on, thinking he is doing the same).
- Change of status forms.
- Tape measure (in case you get that listing call and need to measure the rooms).
- Working flashlight (to find that home in the dark).
- Hammer (to put up your "For Sale" sign).
- *Your name plate* (to attach below the "For Sale" sign).

For Lack Of A Contract Form, A Sale Was Lost

A contract offer can be legally written anywhere. But first you need to have the form. Always carry at least one set with you. One agent had prospects so interested in the house they were viewing that they were ready to make an offer while still in the house. He searched for a contract form but had none and suggested that they all go back to the office. Since the prospects had their own car, they said they would stop for a bite and meet him there later. You guessed it. They talked it over and decided to sleep on it. They never came back. If they had signed the offer at the house, they would then have gone to eat, discussed all the nice things they liked about the house and gone home thinking about "their home," instead of saying to each other: "Do you think we should rush right in and buy, or wait and think about it?"

When the Office Phones Ring

Each telephone inquiry costs a real estate company approximately $50, I am told. Yet many salesmen act as though they cost nothing. A salesman will answer a phone and then hang up saying: "That was only a shopper." A real estate pro knows that shoppers eventually buy. He has gone "shopping" with his wife! Find out what this shopper is looking for. It is possible that no other agent has taken the time to do so.

You should know which listings are being advertised and displayed in your office and inspect them all, if possible. *You need to know your merchandise in order to sell it.* It should not be necessary to ask the prospect on the phone to hold on, while you go around asking and searching. Many lost sales can be traced to the agent not being familiar with the houses listed and advertised.

It is a good policy to withhold the address of the home advertised, when describing it to a phone prospect. Encourage the caller to make an appointment with you, to view the home on the inside as well as on the outside. Don't let him hang up without getting his name and phone number. If he refuses this request, he is probably just a nosy neighbor or some homeowner trying to get comparables for the home he will be putting up for sale. If the phone inquiry is a valid one, let the caller feel important. Give him the impression that you will be dropping everything you have planned for the next few days, to concentrate on finding him the home he seeks.

When the Phones Don't Ring

Sometimes the phones don't seem to ring at all. You have no prospects to work with and the future seems *blah*. Then, when they do ring, it is either another agent calling in for messages, or one from another company requesting information. It may be a homeowner in the process of selling his home himself, wanting to know if his venetian blinds must be included in the selling price. Waiting for the phone to ring is just dealing with lady luck. Create your own luck with your calls to friends and neighbors, for possible referrals. There are many reasons why the phones may not be ringing:

- Time of year. Fewer people move in the winter. Many wait for the children to be out of school to make the change. Others will delay the move until after the holidays (Christmas, Easter, etc.).
- There may be a cutback on jobs in the area.
- The economy may be shaky, and the local buyers and sellers are afraid to move.
- The mortgage money market is bad. Interest rates may be too high and the people have difficulty qualifying for the loan on the homes they would like to buy.

Just Being Busy Is Not Enough

The difference between a productive salesman and a non-productive salesman is what he does with his time. Successful agents make the most of theirs. Just being busy isn't enough. It is being *productively busy* that counts. Don't neglect a good lead while you chase around with a prospect who cannot possibly buy anything now. This prospect may say he'd like to look at homes even though he is unable to buy, but if you know he cannot buy because he is definitely unqualified, remember that it is your time, your gas and your energy that you will be wasting. You should be spending this time in a more productive manner.

A Day Off? What's That?

"The nice thing about being in real estate is that you can get to choose your own hours." That's what I was told. NOT SO! The following reflects what some clients expect:

Monday—6 A.M.: The phone rings and I'm blasted awake.
Hello, is this Charlotte? I didn't wake you, did I? Well, I just wanted to make sure I caught you before you left for the office. (This just happens to be the day that my floor duty starts at 4 P.M.) Incidentally, I tried to get you all day yesterday. (Sunday, and my day off this week.) You weren't home! Don't you go into the office to work anymore?

Monday (same day)—11:30 P.M.: The phone rings and I'm blasted awake.
Hello, Charlotte. You haven't gone to bed yet, have you? I just had to call and couldn't go to bed until I did. I forgot to tell you something this morning. That dimmer switch on the dining room wall— that can remain.

Anytime; any day; any week:
You mean you went away for the weekend with my house unsold? (This client just listed his house the day before and will not be moving for six months, or whenever his home out there gets completed.)

or: I remained home all day Sunday and not even one person came by to show my house. Don't you people work anymore?

You Can't Just Tell Them You're Eating and to Call Back Tomorrow!

My husband has stopped saying: "Tell them to call back, you're eating now" every time the phone rings just as we sit down to dinner. He knows that, like "Pavlov's dog," when the phone rings I drop whatever I am doing and take off. I have learned that time, tide and even the most loyal prospect will wait for no one, once he has finally decided that *he* is ready to go out and look at houses. I have learned that a contract offer written today should be presented today, or there may be another one written, presented and accepted. If I am the lister of a home and get a call telling me that an offer on this house has just been brought into our office, I make every effort to get it right out to the sellers' home for presentation. A contract offer can always be withdrawn and until it is accepted by the seller, is not a valid contract. By the same token, when I write an offer on a house, I want it presented the same day if possible. Tomorrow there may be another, possibly more favorable one presented. Tonight my offer, though lower than the asking price, may be the only one and might be accepted. Sometimes a house remains on the market unsold for months and then three offers are brought in on the same day.

Real estate selling is hard work even though it is exciting. You can't be lazy and make money too. At any rate, I haven't been able to. It's not luck, as some non-productive salesmen will tell you. You have to be the early bird and get there ahead of the next agent. When you hear that a family is planning to move and you know them personally, call on them immediately. If you delay, another "friend of the family" may be more ambitious and get the listing.

One night at about 9 P.M., I received a phone call from a family who had just checked into a local motel. They wanted to set up an appointment with me for the next day at 11 A.M. so that we could look at houses. While talking with them, I learned that they had already made an appointment with another real estate company for 10 A.M. the same day, and were also scheduled to return by plane to their home that evening. I arranged to pick them up at their motel at 8:30 A.M. instead of 11 as they had suggested. As soon as they hung up, I got busy on the phone, setting up early morning showing appointments. The next morning, I was in the office at 8 A.M., making copies of the listed homes I would be showing and picking up the necessary keys. I arrived at their motel as scheduled at 8:30 A.M. to pick them up.

We found just the house they were seeking, and by 11 A.M. were actually writing up a contract offer. I had to remind them to phone the other real estate company to cancel their appointment, which they did. I then set up a 2 P.M. appointment with a lender to have their mortgage application taken at our office, and drove them back to their motel so that they could have some lunch and walk their dog. They were able to make their plane connections with plenty of time to spare and were delighted that they had found a house without becoming completely worn out. (I have since received many referrals from these happy homeowners.)

"Tell them you're eating and to call back tomorrow."

Farm Out the Surplus

After you have been in real estate for some time and are receiving referral and client calls almost daily, you may find that you are unable to handle them all in as competent a manner as you would like. Perhaps you have received a phone call from a prospect who is seeking a house in an area that is some distance from your office, where you are not familiar with the homes. If your company has a branch office in that particular part of town, it is wise to select an agent from that office who will work with you on a referral basis and have this agent try to find a home for your prospect. In this way, you leave yourself free to work with your prospects closer to home and still earn part of the commission on the referral.

No One Ever Told Me There Would·Be Days Like This!

Sometimes you can't help but waste time. In the real estate business anything can happen and it usually does. It might begin with a phone call:

Caller: Hello, may I speak to a salesman?

Me: I am a salesman. My name is Charlotte Korn. With whom am I speaking?

Caller: I am Mr. Homeowner. We will be moving from this area shortly and I'd like some advice.

Me: (Now I'm really excited! "Hey, everyone, keep the noise down!") I'd be delighted to help you. What kind of a house do you have to sell?

Caller: Well, it isn't that exactly. I've already sold my house. Does the oven broiler pan have to be included with the house?

Or another:

Homeowner: Hello, may I please speak to Charlotte Korn?

Me: (A listing call? A prospect? A time waster?) This is Charlotte Korn. Can I help you?

Homeowner: Could you help me sell my house? You sold my neighbor's down the street just three months ago and he raved about you. He told me that whenever I sold my house, not to forget to ask for you.

Me: I'd be delighted to help you. When can I come by?

Homeowner: Well, there's just one thing. I couldn't remember your name, so I listed my house with another real estate company a week ago and they have been doing nothing at all for me. I just remembered your name. Can you please *help them sell my house?*

And the day might end with a walk-in experience, such as the following. One day, a man walked into the office and approached me saying he wanted some information. I couldn't tell, at first, if I was talking to a seller or a buyer, because he asked questions both ways. (e.g., "What would my settlement costs be if I were to purchase a home for $50,000?" And a few minutes later: "What would my settlement costs be if I were to sell a house for $50,000?") I thought that perhaps he was writing an article for a newspaper or doing a school report. I tried to be helpful and answer all of his questions. He thanked me and started to leave. At the door, he turned back to confide that he had just taken a deposit on the sale of his own house from a buyer who had answered his ad, and now, with my help, he knew just how to proceed.

Well, as I said, sometimes there are days like this!

▪ INVESTORS AS CLIENTS

Most of your real estate sales will be to prospects who will move into the house they buy. You will also be approached by investors who realize that real estate is one of the best equity investments. You should be able to turn your well-to-do contacts into real estate investors, once you can demonstrate the benefits to them. This applies to any prospect whose family income is mostly derived from salaries and who pays substantial income taxes (e.g., 30% or more on the last increment of his income). Once you can explain how real estate investors, having the advantages of *leverage, depreciation expense* and *interest expense,* can get a high return (after taxes) on their cash investment, you will be selling second and third properties to some of your prospects.

Why Real Estate Is One of the Best Investments

Historically, in most areas, the value of real property appreciates. Also, net income from an investment in an income producing building

will usually be much greater than net income from other types of investments, having the same safety factor. This is due, mainly, to:

- The special *income tax consideration* that the U.S. Government
  allows to encourage investment in buildings; and
- The *leverage* the investor gains by using borrowed money (the
  mortgage) instead of his own.

Here is a simplified example. You sell a $30,000 single family house
to an investor for 20% down, with an 8%–30 year mortgage, and you obtain a tenant for him for $300 per month. His cash investment is the down
payment of $6,000 plus closing costs, which, in this case, let's say, is
$1,000, or a total of $7,000. His monthly payments (PITI) are $240, and
it will cost an average of $10 per month for maintenance, for the total
cash outlay of $250 per month. His net cash income is $50 per month
($300 rent less cash outlay of $250), which amounts to $600 per year.
At first glance, this seems to be equivalent to only about 8½% of his
$7,000 cash investment, but that is not the entire story.

For income tax accounting purposes, the entire monthly cash outlay, except the small amount paid the lender for principal, is considered
an expense, so that the annual expense for the first year is $3,000, less
$200 in principal payment, or $2,800. In addition, a further expense is
allowed—depreciation expense. In this case, the building worth $25,000
(the $5,000 land value is not depreciable) may be said to have an eco-
nomic life of 30 years, and therefore 1/30 of the $25,000 (or $830) is
deductible as depreciation expense each year. The total expenses, for
tax reporting, are therefore $2,800 plus $830, or $3,630, which results in a
$30 loss when compared to the annual rental income of $3,600.

The cash return of 8½% on the $7,000 investment is said to be "tax
sheltered," because there is no taxable income reported on the property,
but a small loss of $30, which is deducted from the investor's other
income. If the investor, because of his other income, would normally
be paying 50% in taxes on additional income, the tax sheltered 8½% income is equivalent to 17% taxable income, earned from other types of
investments. In many cases, depreciation expenses can be increased
during the early years which results in larger losses (for tax purposes),
and the same cash income. These "losses" when applied against other
income, such as family salaries, result in real tax savings to the investor
who is in a high tax bracket. Also note, that the $200 paid the first year
on principal, is not "spent" by the investor, but increases his equity in
the building by that amount. He will get this back when the property
is sold.

What the Investor Looks For

The investor looks for:

- A good net return on his cash investment (after taxes).
- Appreciation potential for the next 6 to 8 years.

You should therefore be showing him how he can come in with a minimum cash down payment; this gives the highest return, particularly since mortgage interest payments are deductible as expenses. You should tell him what the rental income will be; don't exaggerate this, as you will probably be renting it for him. Then you should point out the features that will make the building saleable later on, and how it may be expected to appreciate in value.

After an investor owns income property for 6 to 8 years, it is profitable for him to sell and take out his appreciation as *capital gains.* This is usually the period when the tax benefits have been lowered, because interest expense has decreased each month (as more of the mortgage is paid off), and the rapid depreciation expense most investors take in the early years results in lower depreciation from the 6th to the 8th year on out. If the property, originally purchased for $30,000, has increased only 3% per year, it would be worth about $38,000 in eight years, which is equivalent to an $8,000 gain on the original $7,000 cash investment (114%), or an average of 9½% for each of the eight years. Income taxes on long term capital gains are at half the normal tax rate. The net annual income (before taxes) for the investor would be this 9½% plus the 17% previously calculated, or 26½% per year. This even beats inflation!

The example given here has been oversimplified. But be assured that the return on investment is not exaggerated. In fact, many properties will show returns on cash investment much higher than 26% per year. Fortunes have been made in real estate by using these same few principles; *High leverage* (i.e., small down payment, big mortgage), maximum *depreciation* expenses, and resale at *appreciated value.* You can help your rich friends and clients by steering them to profitable real estate investments. I have investor clients who own as many as ten income properties. They ask me to watch for any new homes that come on the market, which may be suitable for investment.

Whether a property will appreciate depends upon its *location.* In fact, location is the single most important word in real estate. If the property is located in an expanding suburb, its potential for appreciation is obvious. If the property is located in a neighborhood that is "changing" to a lower income level, there is little chance for appreciation.

You should be aware of the trends in the areas you cover, so that you can advise your investor prospects where to buy. Whenever I think about *location,* I recall the story of three Texans who were standing around at a bar, bragging about their possessions:

First Texan: I own 50,000 acres of farm land and 5,000 head of cattle.

Second Texan: I own 100,000 acres of grazing land and 10,000 head of cattle.

First Texan: (To third Texan) You have been sort of quiet; what do you own?

Third Texan: I guess I can't compete with you fellows. I only own 10 acres, and no cattle.

First Texan: Ten acres? Where?

Third Texan: Downtown Dallas!

So, for investment, the three most important features are *location, location, location.*

Discuss real estate investments with people to whom you have sold homes. They may never have given this a thought. If they show any signs of interest, you can ask them if they have any current investments (stocks, bonds, etc.). Let them know that you are impressed with the fact that they are knowledgeable and familiar with investments. If a prospect has no current investments, and can afford them, you can say: "Don't feel bad—90% of the people have none. It's hard to save money today. You would be surprised at how many do not. A few years ago, if you had bought a house as an investment, it would have been paying for itself (rent) all along, and would have appreciated in addition, as most real estate does." Try to involve his wife: "Men formerly bought investment property without consulting their wives. Now women are more concerned with family affairs. You need to invest while you are working and earning money. If not now, then when?"

Answer their questions, and ask questions of your own, to keep them involved. Give them a reason for buying the property, especially if they are in a high tax bracket: "What do you look for in an investment?" Personally, I look for three things, when I buy an investment house:

- Low down payment. (I don't want to tie up too much cash.)
- A break-even monthly rental cash return where possible.
- A safe and secure investment. (We know that real estate appreciates, and land values go up each year.)

Always recommend that the investor check the tax aspects of a proposed investment with his own accountant. Tax laws change and there are frequent attempts to curb tax shelters. Although the principal tax benefits for real estate investments are usually retained (because Congress encourages such investments), individual investors may be affected differently based on their other investments. For example, some of the tax benefits described in this chapter are considered as "tax preference items." An investor may have tax preference items resulting from his other investments. When the total of all these items exceeds a specified amount during the year, a "minimum tax" (e.g. 15%) is payable on this excess amount.

Co-op With Specialists

My experience has made me expert on selling single family residential units. I have sold many such units to investors. But investors are also interested in apartment houses, commercial property and land. If you are not experienced in these fields and have a prospect who is looking for such property, do as I do—cooperate with an associate agent who specializes. An investor may be seeking undeveloped land to hold for future resale when the suburban population grows out to that location. He may be willing to renovate an older apartment building. Or he may want an older house located on the fringe of an area already zoned for commercial use, using it currently as a rental, but with the intent of eventually replacing it with a business structure. All of these potential investments require keen knowledge of the market conditions in the specific area, awareness of zoning and building codes, of availability of sewers and other utilities, of access to highways, of availability of labor and many other variables. For these reasons, I turn over my investor prospects to the specialists in the types of real property they are seeking.

chapter four

FINANCING

IMPORTANCE OF FINANCING
TO THE SALESMAN

An ambitious real estate salesman should learn all the key elements of financing in order to best serve his buyers and sellers. You do not have to be a financial genius to do this. There are books on the subject. You will be invited to attend seminars. You can keep current on the mortgage market in your area by attending sales meetings, reading all the office notices, getting articles on the subject and discussing financing with your associates in the office. Read the newspapers. Most important, learn where you can get specific information when you need it in a hurry. Lack of knowledge on financing can hurt your sales. Furthermore, if you have "sold" a prospect on a house, but feel bewildered because you do not know how to advise him on its financing, you will lose confidence in your own ability.

If all real estate had to be sold for cash, there would be very few sales and less real estate salesmen. We don't often stop to think how great it is to be able to buy a high-priced house with only a 10% cash down payment, or even no down payment for veterans. The large balance is being financed with a long-term mortgage note. Such liberal financing of homes is not available in most other countries, nor was it always so in the United States.

It was during the great depression of the 1930s that Congress adopted a policy of encouraging home ownership, which it has continued since then. In 1934, the Federal Housing Administration was created to insure home mortgages against default. In 1944, during World War II, the Veteran's Administration was authorized to guarantee mortgages made to veterans. Mortgage loans insured by FHA and VA are two of the most important financing methods for the salesman today. Note that mortgage money is *not borrowed* from FHA or VA. These government agencies insure the lender against loss if the homeowner defaults. With this guarantee, the lender has little or no risk in making mortgage loans for 90%, 95% or even 100% of the property value. Mortgage loans that do not have an FHA or VA guarantee against default, are called conventional loans.

The Mortgage and Promissory Note

The mortgage is a pledge of property to secure payment of a loan. Among other things, it identifies the parties, has the legal description of the property and gives the principal amount of the loan. The promissory note specifies the amount of the loan, the annual interest rate, the number of payments and the amount of each payment. Most residential properties will be financed by a note amortizing the loan over a long period (e.g., 30 years—360 monthly payments) with a fixed monthly payment. The monthly payment includes a payment for interest (which decreases each month) and a payment towards principal (which increases each month) to make a fixed payment each month. Your real estate office will supply you with an amortization book, which permits you to look up the fixed monthly payments for any given principal, interest rate, and number of years for repayment.

You should be aware of two provisions that may be contained in the mortgage note, which may affect your prospect who is borrowing the money for his home:

First: Are the mortgage and note assumable?

If the loan is being made at a relatively low interest rate, it is of benefit to your prospect, the buyer, if it is assumable. It will make it much easier to sell when he decides to do so, because he can pass on to his buyer the benefit of the low interest rate. Also, closing costs on assumptions are much less. Some mortgages are assumable, but only with the permission of the lender. On resale, the lender may permit assumption on condition that the interest rate is changed to a current (higher) one. If the lender does not offer an assumable mortgage loan, there is not much you can do about it except to shop around for another lender, if there is money around for this purpose. Note, however, that when a property is sold on an assumption basis, the original owner remains liable on the note and responsible for payment should his buyer ever default.

Second: Are there any prepayment penalties in the mortgage note?

Some mortgage notes include a provision that the borrower may not accelerate the principal payments more than a specified amount, otherwise specific prepayment charges, usually substantial, must be made. Sometimes these penalties apply only for the first few years of the loan. This affects your purchaser, the borrower, in two ways. Should he have to sell his home next year, it may cost him a significant penalty charge to pay off his mortgage. It could also deter him from refinancing his home, should interest rates decline substantially because of the heavy penalty charges to repay his current mortgage. Some of the "consumer-minded" states have passed laws limiting what the lender can do in making prepayment penalties and non-assumable mortgages. Learn the provisions of any such laws in your own state. Both VA and FHA loans are not permitted to include prepayment penalties, and they are assumable at the original interest rate.

Lenders of Residential Mortgage Loans

Who are the lenders of FHA and VA insured mortgage loans and conventional mortgage loans for homes? Principally, they are savings and loan associations, credit unions and mutual savings banks. These savings institutions find it profitable to borrow money from their depositors at a fixed rate of interest and make long-term residential mortgage loans at a higher rate of interest. Moreover, their charters may require that a given percentage of their assets be held in residential mortgage loans, and there are certain federal income tax benefits to the savings institutions if their major holdings are in residential mortgage loans.

In addition to the savings institutions, commercial banks and insurance companies make substantial amounts of residential mortgage loans, although in most cases, these are handled through mortgage companies—a middle man operation. They accumulate mortgage loans into "packages" large enough to interest these banks and insurance companies. You, the salesman, deal mostly with a savings institution or a mortgage company, and it is convenient to call them all "lenders."

Mortgage Loans As Part of the Money Market

The money needed for mortgage loans is just one of many demands for money in the money market. Some of the important competing demands are:

- Loans to businesses, both short-term and long-term.
- Personal loans including installment loans on autos, furniture, etc., and

■ Government borrowing including federal, state and municipal bonds.

When the supply of money is sufficient, all demands are met and a "normal" (or what is historically considered normal) rate of interest is charged for the use of the money.

Although the total supply of money to meet these competing demands (only one of which is mortgage loans) is limited, it is somewhat under the control of the Federal Reserve Board. By various means at its disposal, the Federal Reserve Board can increase or decrease the total supply of money, to accomplish specific objectives. For example, when the country's economy is behaving normally, the Board tries to increase the money supply in step with the normal growth needs of the economy and population. When there is a threat of runaway price inflation, the Board tries to decrease the money supply to slow down the economy.

How Money For Mortgage Loans Can Dry Up

During an inflationary period, all demands for money increase while the Federal Reserve Board is holding down the supply. This drives up the price for the use of money—that is, the interest rate. Banks that were charging their safest business borrowers a prime rate of 8% interest, may charge as high as 12% interest to these same borrowers. Municipal governments that would normally issue 5% (tax free) bonds to borrow money, have to pay as high as 7% or 8% for similar borrowings. Many people who had their money in safe savings institutions and were getting 5% interest, withdraw their deposits for much higher yields in commercial bank certificates, floating notes, industrial or government bonds, etc. When this happens, the savings institutions have little funds to lend out for mortgages.

The savings institutions, whose major purpose is to make long-term residential loans available, are controlled by government regulations which limit the interest rate they can give their borrowers. Furthermore, FHA and VA, whose purposes are to encourage long-term residential loans at reasonable interest rates, will only guarantee mortgage loans that are made at interest rates they set. When a general shortage of money supply drives interest rates up to (let's say) 10% on conventional loans, the FHA rate, fixed at a lower figure of (let's say) 8½%, will attract no lenders. Because of the limited flexibility of the savings institutions and the FHA and VA interest rate charges, in times of rapid changes, money which was available for long-term residential mortgages, will flow to meet other demands (paying higher interest). Due to circumstances beyond his control, the salesman can find the entire real estate business almost at a standstill. Fortunately, this does not happen too often. When it does, the government usually acts to cool the inflation and bring interest rates down.

Variable Rate Mortgages (V.R.M.)

In order to prevent being squeezed out of the mortgage market during times of inflationary interest rates, some savings institutions are giving mortgages that provide for variable interest rate payments, rather than fixed interest rates. These are called "variable rate mortgages" (V.R.M.) and make it possible for these institutions to compete for savings deposits, by giving a higher interest rate because their V.R.M.s yield a higher return during an inflationary period. In a standard mortgage note, the interest rate is fixed for the entire .period of the mortgage (e.g., 8% for 30 years). In V.R.M.s, the interest rate can go up or down during the long period of the mortgage; the rate movement being tied to an independent index (such as the prime lending rate). There is usually an upward limit of ½ of 1% interest per six month period, and no downward limit. By removing most of the long period risk from the lending institutions, V.R.M.s permit them to offer more attractive initial rates and terms. Your purchaser, the borrower, must be aware that his monthly payments are subject to change, unlike the fixed payments in a standard mortgage.

VA Loans

In 1944, during World War II, the Veteran's Administration (VA) was authorized to guarantee mortgages made to veterans. In this program, a lending institution makes the loan and the VA guarantees the loan up to a certain dollar value. The mortgage loan is guaranteed by the VA but cannot exceed the ceiling currently fixed by Congress (e.g., up to $17,500 or 60% of the mortgage loan, whichever is less). The amount guaranteed and set by the VA, may be changed as economic conditions change. The amount of the loan, however, is not limited by the VA—only the amount of the guarantee. The loan can be for up to 30 years, and the VA guarantees that, in case of foreclosure, they will pay the lender the guaranteed amount in cash. However, in practice, the VA has been paying off the entire balance of the loan to lenders and then arranging for the resale of the foreclosed home. For this reason, VA loans are highly desirable by lenders.

A VA loan is particularly attractive for the veteran, because it requires no money down. In fact, on VA sales, the seller may pay all of the veteran's settlement charges. In order to be sure that the veteran is assuming an obligation within his financial means, the VA has guidelines used by lenders when qualifying the VA buyer. A rule of thumb that you may use is the "60 times formula." If the net effective annual family income is 60 times the monthly payments (principal, interest, taxes and insurance—PITI), that family will undoubtedly be financially qualified. Fifty-five times the monthly payment would be average and 50 times is borderline, but acceptable in many cases. There are some exceptions, however, based on the work and savings record of the veteran. The wife's income is counted if she shows a pattern of work while married. In any event, her income can always be used to offset debts. The VA, however, will consider any reasonable circumstances which might help qualify a veteran.

Points and Loan Fees

Mortgage lenders who are limited in the highest interest rate they may charge by VA regulations (or by state laws or FHA regulations) often find it necessary to obtain more revenue from the loan in order to be able to afford to make the loan. They do this by making a one time charge at the time the loan is made. This is called an "origination fee" and is usually expressed in terms of "points."

The easiest way to understand *points* is to remember that one point is equivalent to 1% of the amount of the mortgage loan. When a house is sold under VA or FHA terms, at a fixed standard interest rate, and if money is scarce, the lenders will require a percentage of the mortgage amount returned to them to induce them to lend out this money. A "point" on a $40,000 loan is therefore $400, and two points would be $800, etc. When points rise suddenly and sharply, a great deal of money can be involved. If a house is sold for $40,000 under VA terms and the purchaser puts down a $10,000 down payment reducing his loan amount to $30,000, the seller will pay points on the mortgage amount of $30,000, or at the rate of $300 per point. Most sellers try to avoid selling their homes under VA or FHA terms, because of the points they will have to pay. (The purchaser under VA or FHA is only permitted to pay one point, no matter how many points are charged to the seller.) Many sellers will specify that their homes be placed for sale only under conventional terms (or assumption, if the loan can be assumed). This is practical when money is available for conventional financing.

Points may be charged on conventional loans also, the limit generally set by state law and varying from state to state. Where the law sets no limit, points may be as high as the traffic will bear. Many states prohibit points on conventional loans.

When mortgage money dries up and there is no conventional financing available (generally because there is a ceiling on the interest rate that can be charged), or if the interest rate soars and prospective purchasers are hesitant to commit themselves, sellers have the choice of not moving at all or of selling their homes under VA or FHA terms (where the interest rate is fixed and generally lower than the conventional rate) and paying the required points, probably netting less than they had hoped for. It is always necessary to explain to the homeowner that points do fluctuate; if they were four when the house was listed, they can go up or down by the time of settlement.

Applying For the VA Loan

The best way to determine if a buyer is eligible for a VA loan is to make application through VA for a certificate of eligibility. Basically, the veteran must be able to prove that he was on active duty for 90 consecutive days, either in World War II or the Korean War, or was on active duty for 181 consecutive days since January 31, 1955. The certificate of eligibility will also show the dollar amount of the guarantee actually available to the veteran (called his "entitlement"). Under some conditions, a veteran who has not completely used his current entitlement, might be eligible to purchase a second home, and if he has sold his current VA financed home, he may be eligible for a reinstatement of his entitlement. However, for any veteran loan, the veteran must occupy the house for which application is being made. It cannot be used as an investment property.

Once you have a valid contract, it is necessary for the veteran to make application for the loan (if he has not already done so). He will need his certificate of eligibility, a copy of the contract of sale and all his employment and bank records, so they can be verified. His application will have to indicate that the cash required for down payment or settlement costs will be readily available. Gift letters from relatives are permitted, but these funds either must be deposited into the purchaser's account, or a verification is required that the donor has the ability to make the gift (or both). If the buyer is relying on funds from the sale of another house, the VA requires that the contract be contingent on the first sale. (This holds even if the contingency is not written into the contract.) In reviewing sources for cash required with your VA prospective buyer, be sure to ask about any cash value of his life insurance, income tax refunds expected, stocks or securities, savings bonds, repayment of loans and any other logical source he may have. Also note that the veteran may borrow money for his down payment and closing costs, but this must be shown as a debt on the loan application.

The VA Appraisal

To be sure the veteran buyer is fully aware of the market value of the home he is buying, the VA requires an appraisal which results in a VA Certificate of Reasonable Value (CRV), which must be shown to the buyer. A contract, written under VA terms, is not valid until the VA has appraised the property and set the value. If the appraisal figure listed in the CRV is higher than the selling price, the contract becomes valid. If, however, the appraisal is for less than the selling price on the contract, the seller and the purchaser must negotiate their differences. A low appraisal can be appealed, and should be supported with at least 3 comparable sales. It is, however, a lengthy procedure.

The VA buyer may pay more than the CRV, but it must be with unborrowed funds, and he must sign a form indicating he has seen the appraisal, is aware that it is for less than the selling price, but that he feels the house is worth the higher figure and is willing to pay that amount. The difference between the CRV and the higher renegotiated selling price, will have to be part of the buyer's down payment.

FHA Loans

In 1934, the Federal Housing Administration (FHA) was created to insure home mortgages against default. The FHA uses government credit to insure the mortgage loans. It does not make the loans. In order to get an FHA guaranteed loan, certain FHA requirements must be met. The buyer must have a cash down payment of minimal amount, as specified by FHA. (If he is also a veteran buying under FHA terms, his down payment requirements are reduced.) Your sales manager can tell you what the current down payment requirement is. For example, a single family home loan (non-veteran) might have a down payment of:

> 3% on the first $15,000 of price
>
> 10% on the next $10,000, and
>
> 20% on any balance (up to a specified maximum price).

On this basis, a house selling for $31,000 and already appraised, would require a down payment of $2,650 as follows:

$450 (3% of first $15,000)

$1,000 (10% of next $10,000)

$1,200 (20% of balance remaining, which is $6,000).

If the buyer does not intend to live in the house, a larger down payment is required.

FHA loans normally are repaid monthly over a 30-year term, providing the house was constructed under FHA inspection procedures. Since FHA insured loans must compete in the money market with other demands, the interest rate fluctuates, but will usually be below the interest rate charged for loans not insured by the government. Added to the interest rate charged, is a fee to cover the cost of mortgage default insurance (e.g., 0.5 percent).

Although most of your FHA financing will be of the type described (called Section 203-b program), you should be aware that FHA has various other financing plans for home mortgages. There are special programs for low and moderate income buyers, which require less of a down payment. There is also a program for servicemen on active duty.

Conventional Loans

Conventional loans are those made by savings institutions and other lenders without government loan guarantees (such as FHA or VA). However, private mortgage insurance (PMI) companies have been willing to insure the lenders against default for a fee. For example, one major PMI company, MGIC (called "magic") covers the top 25% of loan amount against default. This takes most of the risk from the lender, who is then free to offer loans with as low as 5% cash down payment. The cost of the PMI is added to the buyer's monthly payments, or may be paid as a lump sum at settlement.

Terms for conventional loans fluctuate with the money market conditions, even more than do VA and FHA terms, because there is no federal government ceiling on interest rates. For example, when 30 year VA and FHA loans (under 20% down) are being offered at 8½% interest, *plus several points,* equivalent conventional loans with 20% down payment are at 9½% interest; conventional loans with *under* 20% down payment are 9¾% interest, plus PMI of either ½ of 1% per month, or a one time PMI charge of one or two points.

Also, there are usually upper limits placed on the total amount of the loan when buying with less than 20% down. The mortgage market is always changing and rates vary among lenders as well, so you, the salesman, should keep current by reading and noting all bulletins from the lenders, and discussing finance terms with your associates in the office. You can help your purchaser by shopping for the best terms.

For a conventional loan, the purchaser makes application with a savings institution and must meet the credit requirements of that institution. The property is also appraised by the lender. When the lender has approved the loan, it will make a commitment specifying the terms; this should be obtained in writing. In times of rapid market changes, lenders have been known to change their minds if the commitment is not in writing.

The Assumption of Existing Mortgages

One of the best types of contracts for the prospective purchaser is one that provides that he will assume the existing mortgage. If the existing loan is VA or FHA insured, the mortgage is assumable without penalties. If the existing loan is a conventional one, have the mortgage checked to see if it is assumable; some conventional loans have restrictions against assumption. My experience has been that if you ask the lender (and interest rates have risen since the original mortgage was written), he will usually say that assumption is not permitted; so ask an attorney to read the mortgage. Don't write an assumption contract offer without checking. I know many salesmen who have been embarrassed by writing an offer to assume the loan on a house; the offer had to be turned down because the lender did not permit the loan to be assumed. The advantage of an assumption contract is that it permits the purchaser to assume the usually lower interest rate of the original mortgage. Settlement costs are considerably less on an assumption than with most other types of financing. Also, in most cases, the lender does not have to approve the new buyer because the original owner remains contingently liable if the new owner should ever default.

On an assumption, the difference between the selling price and the mortgage amount being assumed is the cash down payment that is required. Sometimes, this can be much more than the 5% or 10% down that your purchaser would like to make. Remember, if the interest rate on the original mortgage is not significantly lower than the current rate, there is no real advantage in an assumption sale; a new mortgage, particularly one under FHA or VA terms, would require a smaller down payment and be amortized over a longer period (probably 30 years).

Second Mortgage or Second Trust

Sometimes the prospective buyer has an opportunity to assume an excellent first mortgage with low interest rate and low monthly payment, but the cash down payment is more than he can handle. The seller, too, would prefer an assumption sale, because it makes the sale more desirable where the interest rate is low. This, in turn can be reflected in the higher price he can command. Such sales can be worked out by having the seller take back a second mortgage (in some states, called a second trust) in order to lower the cash down payment required. For example, if a $20,000, 6% mortgage remains on the house being sold for $30,000, and the purchaser can only afford a $4,000 down payment, the seller may be willing to hold a second mortgage for $6,000 which would be paid over a given term (say 10 years), with constant monthly payments of principal and interest. In this way, the buyer takes advantage of the 6% interest rate on $20,000 of his loan, and pays the current interest rate on only $6,000 of his loan. If the sale was not made by assumption and second mortgage, the buyer would have to pay the current interest rate on the entire loan. You should, however, advise your client that should he take back a second mortgage and later suddenly be in need of cash, he can probably sell it, but at a discount from the current value.

Some sellers like the idea of a steady monthly income over many years, and a second mortgage can be attractive to them. There can also be a substantial income tax saving to the sellers under these terms because the sale may be considered as an installment sale. For example, if in this $30,000 sale, the home originally was purchased for $18,000, the seller has a $12,000 long-term capital gain to report as income in the year of the sale. Even though this is taxed at half his tax rate, it is added to his other income and could be substantial, depending on his tax bracket. On the other hand, if the mortgage is assumed with a second trust and the actual cash received during the year of sale is less than 30% of the selling price, the sale is treated, for tax purposes, as an installment sale, and the $12,000 long-term capital gain (still taxed at half his tax rate) is spread over the entire term of the second mortgage (10 years in this example) being paid only in proportion to the amount of principal repayment received each year.

Second Trust With Balloon

When you are working out an assumption contract offer with a second mortgage, you have to be sure that the buyer can handle the total of both monthly payments. The first mortgage payments consisting of principal, interest, taxes and insurance (PITI) to the lender and the second mortgage payments to the seller. You can have some flexibility with the second mortgage payments by increasing the number of years in the term of the second mortgage. For example, you find that if the second mortgage was for a term of 15 years, the payments would come out just right for the purchaser. But the seller wants to be paid off before 15 years; he insists that the note be completely paid in 7 years. This can be handled by making the second mortgage payments equal to those of a 15 year mortgage, but at the end of 7 years, the complete balance is due in a lump sum payment (the balloon payment). This may frighten some prospects who will wonder where they would get the needed cash at the end of the seventh year. But there are two things to consider: (1) People move and there is a good chance that the house will be sold again within seven years; and (2) the first mortgage is decreasing each year, and the house probably appreciating, so that before the seventh year, the first mortgage loan probably can be refinanced for another long period, and the second mortgage paid off. You will find that your investor prospects will often use second mortgages, amortized over long periods, but payable in 5 to 10 years, with a balloon payment. They are usually interested in lowering their cash payments, and are sophisticated enough to realize that they can sell or refinance the house before the balloon payment is due.

The Wrap-Around Mortgage

Where a low interest mortgage exists, but is not assumable, it is possible for the seller to continue to make payments on his first mortgage and give the purchasers a new mortgage—called a wrap-around mortgage—for the entire amount they wish to have financed. This can only be done under certain circumstances, and it is best to consult your attorney, in advance, if a wrap-around mortgage can help close your sale.

The Cash Sale

At some time in your real estate career, you might have an elderly couple as prospects and they will want to pay all cash for their home. They have saved the amount needed over many years, or just sold a house in which they had substantial equity. Their current income is low, perhaps from retirement benefits and social security payments and they would like to keep their current housing payments low. What could be better for them than to own a paid-up home, where all they are required to pay are the real estate taxes and insurance each year.

The Trade or Exchange

When a homeowner sells his home and moves into a new one of equal or higher value, within a time period specified in current tax laws (e.g., 18 months), the homeowner does not have to pay any capital gains tax on the profit he made in the sale of his home. Should an investor, not living in the home, sell one house and buy another, he is still liable for capital gains tax on the profit he made on the sale of his first house. However, the income tax law permits the investor to make a direct exchange for a home of equal or higher value, without capital gains tax. This is called a "trade" or "exchange" and you will find it useful for your investor clients.

chapter five

SELLING HOMES

■ HOW TO QUALIFY THE PROSPECT QUICKLY AND PROFESSIONALLY

When a prospect comes in to buy a home, it is important to quickly determine whether, in fact, he is qualified. Find out:

- What *he thinks* he wants,
- What *he can actually afford,* and
- What *you think is right* for him.

A young couple may walk into the office, slightly confused. You need to sit them down, relax them with your friendly manner; offer them some coffee or a soft drink, and *start asking questions.*

Since time is money, a good salesman does not waste it. He knows that *most home buyers are impulse buyers* and that every sale is a bit different from every other one. He knows that a buyer may describe exactly what he wants and then turn around and buy a home that is the complete opposite. I showed colonial-styled homes to a family who requested one with a two-car garage and ended by selling them a modern ranch-styled home with a carport. They saw it as we drove by, fell in love with it and offered for it.

Some buyers walk into the office with a newspaper in which they have circled a number of real estate ads, or with a notebook filled with addresses and information on homes they would like to inspect or have already visited. One couple walked in one day while I was on duty. They had a black looseleaf notebook that was as complete as our office ad book. Ads were pasted on each page, with notations alongside describing the newspaper source, the date of the ad, and the reaction of the couple to the ad. They had seen them all.

People have various reasons for buying a particular home. It is important to discover their reasoning, and eventually to satisfy their needs, if you are to make the sale. Some prospective purchasers love a challenge and will purchase a run-down property for the thrill and fun of fixing it. Others will want a home that they can "move right into without having to do a thing." Listen for the little things that clue you to their real desires and then keep alert for signs of developing interest as you show homes.

Don't Pre-judge

Don't assume that a man has no money because he walks in looking as though he has just come in from the mines. He may just be the owner of that mine! On the other hand, the well-dressed couple who pull up in that snappy sports car, dressed as though they could afford to buy anything, may be wearing all that they actually own; their car may be heavily mortgaged or it may belong to a parent. Sometimes, even though your prospects don't have much funds of their own, daddy owns a bank and is willing to finance the couple, as soon as they find their dream house.

Here is an example of how looks can be deceiving: I had prospects looking for a particular high-priced home. What I thought was the right home for them, came through as a new listing and I phoned them immediately. She was in the kitchen doing the dishes and he was raking leaves in the yard. I said: "Come as you are, this home won't last," and they did. They loved the outside as we drove up and a quick walk through convinced them. Since they were on limited time, we rushed back to the office and I started to write the offer. As they were signing the papers, Mrs. Homeowner called me to complain about the quality of the prospects I had just brought over: "You know that little couple can't afford to buy this house!" I told her that if she and her husband would stay home for about a half hour, I would be over with an excellent contract offer. It was an all cash offer!

Ask the Right Questions

You would be surprised at how many agents will chauffeur prospects around all day and then let them walk out of the office without getting their names and phone numbers. Make sure you ask the right questions at the start. You may be wasting the entire day and lose other sales, if you do not do so. Here are some of the questions you might ask:

- How large a home are you looking for?

- When do you need it?
- Is there any special area you prefer?
- What special features do you require? (fenced yard, garage, fireplace, carpeting, style of home, etc.)
- Do you own the home where you are presently residing? Has it been sold? Settled? When do you have to give possession? (If it has not been put on the market for sale: Do you need to sell in order to buy now?)
- Do you have your home listed with a REALTOR? Has an appraisal been ordered?
- If renting, are you on a lease? When does it expire?
- What is your present salary? Is your wife employed? How much is she earning?
- How much of your savings do you plan to invest? (Don't jar their ego by saying: "How much cash do you have?")
- Do you have any outstanding debts? Car payment?
- Have you looked at any homes in this area? Seen anything you liked?
- Are you a veteran? (If prospect wants to purchase under the G.I. bill.)

You should be on a first name basis with your prospects after a few short minutes. The sooner they are at ease with you, the sooner they will consider you as a friend and adviser. You need to be sincere in your desire to be of help. *Impress your name* on your prospects. "Remember to ask for Charlotte Korn—that's spelled like 'sweet corn' but a 'K'." Many a commission has been lost because a prospect could not remember the name of the agent he came in to see.

Determine Urgency

Most agents have at least one prospect who calls about once a week saying: "Have any new listings come in since I last spoke with you, that are bargains?" This prospect is looking for a terrific buy in a choice area. He is hoping that a house will be listed where the seller is desperate and will give his home away. Of course, no one is that desperate and it hardly ever happens. (If a seller is desperate and is willing to sell his home as a bargain, there is always a real estate broker willing to guarantee the sale, who will list the house.) This bargain-hunting prospect is obviously not in a hurry to buy.

If a prospect calls saying he is thinking of moving when he finds a home that is larger and better than his present one, and where he can make an even exchange, he is just dreaming. If a prospect who can only afford a small, inexpensive home, insists that you show him estates with acreage (he describes Mount Vernon), you again have a dreamer. With such a prospect, there is no urgency, and your chances of ever selling him a home are slight. This prospect is just "chasing that elusive rainbow" and you should allocate little of your time to him. If a prospective purchaser has just been transferred to your part of town and is staying in a motel, with his furniture on the way, you have an excellent chance of selling him a home if you find one that suits his needs. If such a prospect phones saying he would like to come right out to look for a home, don't try to put him off because it is raining or because you are not in the mood today. If you ask him to wait for another day, he may set up that appointment with you, but immediately call another real estate office to set up an appointment to "come right over." You will later discover that he has already purchased a home, when the day for your appointment arrives.

Let the Prospect "Do the Walking"

You have just spent the day driving prospective purchasers all over town, and shown them all the local listings. You find that they like what they have seen in the homes, but are not sure this is the area for them and want to look elsewhere before they come to a final decision. You should then give them a map, route it for them, and give them a list of addresses of homes for sale along the way. Advise them to drive around, look for signs by other REALTORS, copy the names and addresses together with the phone numbers, and report back to you. You can then phone these real estate companies for additional information as to room size, price, etc. They will love doing this, because they will feel they are not being pressured for an immediate decision. For your part, they are using their time and gas, and doing the legwork. If your relationship is sound, they will return and probably buy the house you thought was right for them on the first day.

Recognize the Non-buyer

When a couple walks into the real estate office and the woman does all the talking, it is natural to direct all your answers to her. The man may be very quiet, offer no comments and ask no questions. He may look away when you display the floor plans. The woman may tell you

"We want a large colonial with acreage, no money down, and low monthly payments. Our income? $10,000 a year."

that she makes all the decisions and her husband agrees to anything that she wants. He may even nod meekly. *Don't believe it!* You may drive them around all day, show them every house in the book and she may love them all. When you think it is all wrapped up and you try to close the sale, she *lowers the boom.* She says: "I have to talk it over with my husband" and they leave. When you phone the next day, she tells you that her husband doesn't want to move but she does and that she is "working on him." She goes on to say that he actually didn't want to look at homes but went along for the ride to please her. "You were really wonderful and I love that last home but I will have to call you back as soon as I can talk him into it. And again—thanks for being so nice and helpful." So much for that "sale." It is important to remember that *you must have the desire of both husband and wife in order to close a sale.*

These are usually indications that your prospects are not buyers:

- A couple drives up. The man comes into the office and asks questions about the houses listed for sale in the area. His wife refuses to leave the car (and she is in excellent health). Here you can only accomplish one-half of a sale. Which means NO SALE.

- A couple walks into the office together, sit down, and lets you describe all the homes that are available. However, they don't seem to be talking to each other. They may glare at each other in anger. One-half of this pair is there under protest, and will probably refuse to consider any home, even if it is the right one for them.

- A couple walks into the office together. They are friendly and talk to each other. Both are equally interested in the homes that are listed for sale. However, both keep glancing at their watches and giving each other knowing looks and signals which you notice, if you are alert. Before you make your first phone call to arrange for a showing, they let you know that they are allowing you one-half hour to find their dream home, since they have set up appointments on the hour for the rest of the day and will be looking in other areas; that this is their first stop and please hurry.

- A couple comes into the office.

  1. They have no money, no job (or one with a minimal salary), and no prospects for future raises.

  2. They won't give you their names or phone numbers, and when you insist, say they don't want to be pressured by real estate

agents. Sometimes they give you a fictitious name or phone number.

3. They refuse to discuss finances. (Here you have to "read the prospect." Some prospective purchasers are just suspicious, and will warm up and give you this information if handled patiently.)

4. They insist you give them names and addresses of every home listed, so they can drive around on their own and look at the homes. They assure you that after they have done so, they will return to your office, seek you out personally, and buy a home from you. *Don't believe it!*

You may think you have a genuine buyer. He asks all the right questions about the house you just showed and wants to know where the schools, shopping, churches and parks are. You give him the information and knock yourself out showing him all around the area. You think he and his wife are ready to sign an offer and can't wait to get to the conference table fast enough. And then they tell you, confidentially, that they actually wrote an offer yesterday, on the type of home they had requested you show them. It was directly with a homeowner who gave them until today to make their final decision. They had not been sure about living in this area and wanted to see it all. Now that you have shown them around and pointed it all out to them and were so kind, giving them all the information, they were convinced that they were going to love living here. They have decided to buy that house from the homeowner right away. Aren't you just delighted for them?

Many people make a hobby of inspecting houses each Sunday, after lunch. They have been doing this for years. Find out how long your prospect has been house-hunting. When I was a rookie agent, I drove around each Sunday for weeks, with the same middle-aged sweet couple, who told me they were "cash buyers." Each Sunday morning when they arrived, I would think: "This is the day that they will finally buy a home." Each Sunday evening before they drove off, they would set up an appointment to "come out next Sunday, and we will look at homes again." I finally was fed up and surprised them by telling them I had a showing appointment for the following week. They looked hurt and bewildered but said they would call me later that week. They never did. This couple knew every house in the area and could tell the age of each by the flooring. They knew the yearly price increases on each and every house. They had been looking for a home since forever.

It is not too difficult to recognize a non-buyer. The trick is to do it quickly. I once took a well-qualified couple out to look at some homes.

Prospect reading owner signs.

The man sat in back with a notebook on his lap and was busy making notations as we drove along. I could see him in the rear view mirror. The thing that disturbed me was that he was doing too much writing for someone who had not yet inspected the first house on my list. I took another look and there he was, trying to look out of both the right and left windows at the same time, searching for signs on front lawns proclaiming "For Sale by Owner," and busily scribbling down these addresses and phone numbers. When we returned to the office, he thanked me and left saying he had plenty of time left on his lease and wanted to do some looking on his own. (I thought he had already done plenty of that on my time, but of course, I didn't say so.) I thanked them for coming out. You never can tell. He may need a chauffeur again and perhaps the next time I can route them another way.

Would you have recognized this non-buyer? One rainy New Year's Eve, I had floor duty from 1 P.M. to 4 P.M. I· was anxious to get home before it started snowing. At 3:30, a young woman phoned and asked to speak to an agent. I tried to sound helpful:

She: What kind of an area is Westmore? (A small housing area close to our office.)

Agent: It's a lovely area. What kind of a house are you looking for?

She: Well, that doesn't matter. I just want to know about *that area.*

Agent: We have some three and four bedroom homes there. What price range are you interested in?

She: Well, that really doesn't matter. I just wanted to *see* the area. Can you come by now and pick me up and drive me around *that area.* I am staying at my mother's house and my husband has the car. (I learn that her mother's house is more than twenty miles from our office.)

Agent: Can you make a decision to buy without your husband?

She: I never do *anything* without my husband. You don't understand. My husband took the car and is looking for a job. We are staying with my mother and I am without wheels. My mother knows of a house for sale by an owner in that area and I wanted to drive around and see what it looks like. If my husband gets the job here, then I can decide whether we want to consider living there. (She paused for a moment, and then added as an afterthought:) Of course, I'll be sure to call you if I don't like that area. Then, when we return next month, you can drive us around while we look at other areas to see where we would like to settle.

Agent: How about tomorrow? (I haven't given up yet!) Then I
        can take both of you around to look at the homes together.

She: That will be impossible. We're returning home tomorrow
        and aren't sure when we'll return. It has to be *now*.

I begged off that one.

Don't Spin Your Wheels

Many salesmen believe that because they are working hard, they
will surely succeed. Not so. Make sure that what you are doing is con-
tributing to your progress and not just "making work." Rushing around
without a firm game plan is just a waste of time. Don't chase around with
prospects, showing them homes they cannot buy. For example, if you have
a definite VA buyer, who only has enough money for settlement costs,
don't show him homes that can only be bought on an assumption basis,
with a large down payment.

If the prospects refuse to drive to the homes with you, but want
to take their own car, they may be thinking of leaving you immediately
after they have seen the homes you intend to show and probably have
no thought of buying now. Always try to get the prospects to drive with
you, telling them that you want to point out the places of interest along
the way. If the man prefers to drive for a valid reason (e.g., a sleeping
baby in the back) go along with them in their car. It is important to be
in the same car, because you can listen to their comments going to
the homes and returning to the office. You can also do some additional
qualifying of the prospects along the way. Finally, they have to return
to the office because they have to get you back. Sometimes, during this
ride back to the office, you can discuss the attractive features of the
home you thought was right for them, and close the sale at the office.

Avoid showing those homes on which you know an offer has
already been written or where one is being countered. Sometimes an
offer exists that has a contingency or kick-out clause and the lister of
the property will tell you that this sale will never be consumated because
the purchaser will probably never sell his home (or get the gift letter,
etc.) in order to remove his contingency. You then write a secondary
offer on the house only to find out that the purchaser on the primary
offer somehow managed to sell his home overnight or has just inherited
a bundle and removed his contingency. Once your prospects had decided
on this house and convinced themselves that this was "their dream house"
and then had to lose it because of the primary offer being accepted, the
chances are very slim that they will be satisfied with any other house
you show them. You have probably lost a good prospect.

As soon as you realize that you have non-buyers, don't waste any further time. Don't feel obligated to drive them around just because they ask you to. Instead explain that you will keep in touch with them and when their financial status changes, other homes will be available and you will gladly show them those houses. I learned a valuable lesson in my first year in real estate; one that I never forgot. The prospect call I received as I was sitting down to dinner one evening started me rushing to the car. I arrived at the office a few minutes before the prospects, made three phone calls to the homesellers whose homes I would be showing, and off we went in my car while there was still daylight. This was a young couple who were looking for a ranch style house and wanted to assume the loan. They told me that they had a friend living locally and they knew exactly what they wanted. She was expecting a baby and they wanted to move into their home as soon as possible. As we started off, I began to qualify them: "How much do you plan to invest?" His answer nearly floored me. "Why nothing. I just wanted to assume somebody's loan and take over the payments." He had no money at all!

I pulled over to the side of the road, stopped the car, turned to him and asked the questions that I should have asked on the phone at home:

Q. Are you a veteran?
A. No.
Q. How much are you earning?
A. With my bonus?

It turned out that they were not married, both were underage, and he didn't earn enough to qualify to buy a camper. My advice to them was to find a sympathetic relative and move in, and then start saving their money. I returned home to a cold dinner.

A professional agent selects his prospects carefully, and qualifies them before he spends substantial time with them. The rookie sometimes takes off immediately, and can drive his prospects around all day before discovering that they are not qualified. A rookie can get a lift out of just showing homes, but a professional looks for results.

▪ SHOWING AND TELLING

Will the Real Boss Please Stand Up!

In order to make a sale, it is necessary to take immediate command of the situation. *Determine who makes the decisions.* The one who does most of the answering to your questions, is probably the dominant one.

If you are in doubt about who the boss is, ask a question such as: Shall we now look at some of the other houses?" The "boss" will give you your answer. Sometimes the dominant one does not talk much. He only speaks up where it counts.

A woman comes into the office to look at homes and she is alone. She tells you that she does all the screening since "my husband doesn't like to look at homes (or doesn't have the time) and what I like, he likes." This may actually be the case, but it is rare. I have written offers where the woman came out, found the home she liked and then phoned her husband to leave work early to see it. I once wrote a contract offer, had the woman sign it and give me a check for the escrow, with instructions to call at her home that evening for her husband's signature. He signed without even inspecting the house. Just be aware that sometimes a bored housewife is looking for a change of scenery and a free ride. She may even ask you to pick her up at home, since she has no car. It doesn't take long for a pro to recognize this non-buyer.

Sometimes a man will tell you he desires a colonial style house. His wife says she wants a ranch style. Listen to the conversation. Don't volunteer any opinions but show both styles of homes. They may surprise you and both decide on a split level home. Try to direct your attention to the dominant member, but don't neglect the other. Watch them and listen carefully. Soon the dominant member will start doing the selling for you. Incidentally, if you are a female agent, it is a good idea to place the woman in the front seat of your car with the man in the back seat, when driving out to look at the homes. If she is the jealous type, she may resent being relegated to the back seat, where she cannot hear all of the conversation. When he finally says: "Darling, what did you think of that house?" don't be the one to answer for "Darling."

Learn to Read Your Buyers

There may be one feature above all that a prospect wants in a home. As soon as he sees this feature in a house, he will want to make an offer, even if other features are negative.

I drove one family around all day looking for a home to suit their needs. There were some lovely ones that I thought were right for them, but something seemed to be missing. I couldn't get them excited enough to make a written offer. We were all tired and the woman was still searching. Then I heard her say to her husband: "If only the last house we saw was yellow with brown shutters. It looked so drab." I told her the house could always be painted but she said "No—it has to hit me right." There was one listing I had not bothered to show them since it had all the wrong features—wrong, that is, except for the outside paint-ing. It was painted yellow and had brown shutters. We turned the car around and headed for this house and they made a full price offer for it on the spot.

Learn to understand what motivates the people who come out looking for a house. Develop an empathy with them. Try to put yourself in their place and you will anticipate their needs. Demonstrate your interest and sympathy. Look for the buying signals. Then read between the lines of what they say.

"Do you have a three bedroom house with a garage—one that is air conditioned?" they ask when they walk into the office. "It has to be priced under $30,000 and we have looked everywhere." You look through your listings and try to select what you think they want, but they have seen them all. They have been looking for months and inspected every home listed in the area that was priced under $30,000. Your next move should be to ascertain if there is any way that they can possibly qualify for a home in a slightly higher price range and then show them those homes. No one has thought to show them anything over their $30,000 limit and one of these houses may be the one they want and result in a sale. Some prospects are afraid to tell you how much they can afford to spend. They will tell you $30,000 hoping to get a $35,000 home at a bargain price. They could be right. Sometimes a house that is listed for $35,000 may have an anxious seller sitting in it, with his furniture already packed, who will gladly accept an offer under his listed price. You can also assume that many purchasers do not reveal all their assets. When they see a home they like, they can suddenly find a source of extra money for the down payment.

Put your own preferences aside. You may not like a particular house you are showing, but do not assume that your prospects feel as you do. One home I showed a young couple had a hill in back, suitable for goat climbing, but they loved its privacy and started planning a terraced garden as soon as they saw the back yard.

You can best read your prospects when they are relaxed. If you are seated, they should be leaning forward, listening to every word you say. If you find the attention of the woman wandering, you will need to direct your next question to her and call her by name. If she is tense and stiff, and is hanging on to her purse or gloves for dear life, you know something is bothering her. If you don't find out what it is, you will be wasting valuable time. A woman may sit and let her husband do all the talking but she will be listening to all that is said. You want her agreement. You can only hope that she is one of those people who can make a fast decision and when she finally does speak, it will be to say: "I like it—how about you?" Try to maintain "eye contact" with

"Sorry—in this town, the $20,000 house you want sells for $60,000."

your prospective buyers throughout the conversation. When the prospect looks away, it can only mean that he is thinking of a way to say "no" or is trying to plan an escape. You will, no doubt, run across these "types" of prospective buyers:

The know-it-all ■ Let him brag and congratulate him on his decisions.

The smart alec ■ He may be in and out of the property while you are still introducing him at the door. Let him run himself down until you feel he has run out of steam.

The dead pan ■ Says nothing. Answers your questions with grunts or monosyllables. Find something in common to talk about with him—the neighborhood, his hobby, anything.

Henpecked husband ■ Says "yes, dear" to everything his wife says. Ask him directly: "Your wife says this house is perfect. *How do you feel about it?*"

The slow guy ■ Let him take all the time he needs. Don't rush him.

Likes everything ■ This man is probably afraid to rely on his own judgment. Get him to confirm your thinking by agreeing with you on one point at a time.

Chatterbox ■ Never try to outtalk him. Just wait until he says something that you would like to explore, and then say: "Now that is most interesting (or important)." He will probably stop to review what it was that he said, and that is your opportunity.

Skeptic ■ Get him to agree with you on minor points. When he does not, ask him why. Use documented material, if possible, in order to convince him.

Stubborn ■ Compliment him on his opinion and firm stand. Tell him you would be doing the same thing in his place. Never force him into a corner. You will convince him yet.

Meet You at the Office

Always arrange for the prospects to meet you at your office, if possible. The only time you will want to vary this is when they are from out of town, staying at a nearby motel and have no means of transportation. You can then arrange to pick them up, take them to your office, make your showing appointments and hopefully write a contract offer. There are many advantages in having prospects come directly to the office. You can qualify them before you start showing houses and also get better acquainted with them on the drive to the homes. By the time you reach the first one, you should be friends.

If you arrange to meet the prospects at a particular house location, they may get there before you do, look at the outside, not like what they see and keep on driving. When you arrive a few minutes later, you may think they have not yet arrived and wait for them in the cold. You will not only have frozen feet waiting, but will probably have lost the prospects as well. If you had taken them in your car from the office and they were not too impressed with the outside of the house, courtesy would have required that you view the interior since the appointment had been set. They might have become so enchanted with the interior that they would have told you how easily they could "make the lawn over into a green carpet."

Setting the Conversational Stage

In order to sell successfully, it is important for the agent to control the conversation and to channel the buyer's thinking towards achieving the sale. The professional agent thinks positively and assumes success. He is enthusiastic and his attitude rubs off on his prospects. When he gets excited, they get excited right along with him. When he assumes the sale, his attitude infects the prospects and they accept it as a foregone conclusion. He is careful in the terms he uses. It is an "established home" you are showing, not a "used house." It is a "terrific value" not a "cheap house."

In order to sell effectively, you need, first of all, to:

1 ■ *Get your prospect's attention:* If you do not have his attention, he will not be listening to you. Call him by name. If you are not sure you have it right, don't hesitate to ask him how it is spelled and pronounced. Write it down phonetically if it is a difficult one and master it. Since it is the word he most enjoys hearing, if you call him by name in a warm, friendly manner, he will naturally have a warm, friendly feeling towards you.

You can start by talking to him briefly about something that he is interested in, such as his family or hobbies. However, since attention is only a temporary state, it is necessary to develop it into interest. You can usually tell if you are holding his attention. If he starts looking around the room while you are talking, or whispers to his wife and looks at his watch, you know you are losing him. He may even yawn in your face. To recapture the prospect's attention, you might ask a leading question or just do something physical, like dropping a book. Try stopping in mid-sentence. That will get to him. He will turn to you in surprise. Now ask your leading question.

2 ▪ *Keep his interest:* Continue calling him by name as you point out the favorable features along the way or when asking a specific question. He will listen avidly to all that you say if he thinks there will be some benefit or advantage to him in what you say.

3 ▪ *Build his desire:* Your own enthusiasm and confidence will work wonders in doing this. Desire is purely emotional and if you have built up a strong enough desire for ownership in your prospect, he should be ready to act.

4 ▪ *Now get him to act:* The most effective way to get a prospective purchaser to act is to start asking questions to which he will answer "yes." If you have properly set the stage with your own enthusiasm, your prospect will follow your lead and be ready to act by signing a contract offer.

Avoid the memorized "sales pitch." It sounds artificial. Be yourself and put your prospect at ease. Be self-confident throughout and always sincerely interested in his needs. Always try to see his point of view. Remember to stress the positive benefits that he will derive from home ownership.

How to Recognize Those Buying Signals

Some prospects after seeing the home they want can make a fast decision; others need to come back again and again, and will tend to resist any situation that requires them to make a major decision. The two obstacles to overcome are fear and indecision. A professional makes it easy for the buyer to say "yes" without thinking too much. Your attitude plays an important role in motivating the buyer. If you provide an environment which can only lead to positive actions and results, you will end with a signed contract offer, and the sale.

Ask friendly, inquiring questions in order to get this "yes" response. The sale should follow automatically as a result of a series of events, which you have arranged. Be confident and assume that they will be buying. Show it in your manner. Avoid straining the prospect's thinking processes, and *never argue*. If he has objections, you will want to know about them as soon as possible, so that you may try to turn them into advantages by showing the prospect all the benefits he will derive from ownership of this house. Once you get the prospect to agree on simple things (e.g., "Do you like this area?") and have him saying "yes" frequently, it will become difficult for him to even think "no." Yet, it is also important not to oversell the virtues of a particular house. If for some reason you cannot close on that one and the prospect has already identified himself and his family with it, you may be unable to sell him on another.

Save Time By Phoning for Showing Appointments, In Advance

You can save yourself time and energy by making your showing appointment call well in advance, such as follows:

Hello Mrs. James. I am Charlotte Korn with P.G.P. Real Estate Company. Is your home still being offered for sale? (I want to make sure it has not been sold.) I wonder if I may come over this afternoon to show your home to a prospective purchaser. I expect them in our office about 2 P.M. and we should be there about 3 P.M. However, please assume that we will not be coming out if we are not there by 3:30 P.M. They may decide to come at a later date and in that event I will call back at a later time. Thank you.

When the prospect does come into the office, you will not have to stop to make any phone calls to set up appointments. Also, should the prospect decide on a home before you have shown them all, you do not need to drop everything to call an irate homeowner who has been sitting at home expecting you. She knows that if you are not there by 3:30 P.M., you will probably not be coming over. You can concentrate all your attention on closing the sale.

Know the Homes You Plan to Show

Select, with care, the homes you plan to show to your prospect. Being familiar with the physical features is not enough. You need to know the terms and conditions under which the homes are being offered. When is the house available? Is the mortgage assumable? If it can be assumed, what is the interest rate; the loan balance; the monthly payment? Is the owner anxious? If your office does not have this information, do not hesitate to call the lister of the property, even if he works for a cooperating broker. Ascertain if the house is being offered under VA or FHA terms; if an appraisal has already been ordered, and the appraisal value, if it has been received. Find out if the price is firm. Each agent is anxious to sell his own listing and should be glad to answer your questions. When you know all these things before showing the homes, you save yourself much legwork. Too many agents have come into our office to pick up a key in order to show one of our listings and then returned the key saying: "My people loved that house! Has the VA appraisal come in yet?" only to find out that the house was not being offered under VA terms. You should personally inspect the homes you intend to show even though you have seen them previously. Sometimes the sellers have made changes and on another visit, you can ascertain this.

Showing the "Open House"

If you are planning to show any open houses to your prospects, make sure that you identify yourself and the office you represent to the agent who is holding the house open. *Never send an unescorted prospect to another REALTOR's open house.* If their agent sells your prospect the house, *he* is entitled to the full commission. You are, in effect, presenting that agent with a "live prospect." Sometimes you can work out a commission split with another agent from your own office when he holds a company listed house open, or arrange to give him a referral fee if your prospect buys the house. Be sure to arrange this in advance and log your prospect in at the office. Give the prospect your card, with written directions to the house on the reverse side. Remember, however, that you take a chance when you send a good prospect out to inspect an open house without going along. He may see another one being held open by another real estate company and like that one better. If you had been with him, you could have escorted him through that one, written up the offer, and earned the commission.

Actually, showing open houses has many advantages. The house is probably in its best show condition and usually without anxious sellers around. Also, there is no need to phone in advance for an appointment, nor do you have to arrange for key pickup. You know the hours it is being held open—usually from 1 P.M. to 5 P.M., and can just drive up while showing other houses to your prospects. A word of caution: It is obviously unethical to solicit new clients or prospects in or around any house being held open by other agents.

The Negative Tenant

From time to time a house comes on the market with excellent terms and conditions. It is in good repair and in a good location, and yet remains unsold. When you try to show this house, you find out why. The tenants do not want the house to be sold. They do not want to move. They will not allow a key to be placed in the listing office. They do not want anyone in the house when they are not home. They either absent themselves on weekends or just don't answer the phone. If you are lucky and catch them in when you phone for a showing appointment, there is always some excuse: "I was just walking out the door and don't know when I'll be back," or "No, it can't be shown today. I have a sick headache," or "No, I can't stay home for another five minutes. I am already late for an appointment." I had such a listing at one time, and solved the problem. I described the interior to my prospect and showed him the exterior. I knew the tenants were home although they had not answered the phone nor the doorbell. We then returned to the office and I wrote a contract offer with the following contingency: "Contingent on purchaser's inspection of the interior of the home within two days from the date of acceptance of this offer." I phoned the sellers and got their acceptance of the terms of the offer. They, in turn, phoned the tenants that they were coming over to see them, and we all went along. (P.S. The purchaser removed the contingency as soon as he saw the interior. It was exactly what he wanted.)

Remember Their Emotional Needs

People buy homes with their emotions. It is important to remember this and to keep the following needs of the purchasers in mind:

- Their need for recognition.
- Their love of family, and their pride.
- Their desire for personal and financial security.
- Their peace of mind.
- Desire for romance and excitement.
- Their personal well-being, and their health.
- Their desire to make a change.
- Location of the home.
- Convenience to work, shopping and schools.

There is a "secure" feeling that goes with home ownership, since it is a tangible asset, not just a piece of paper, such as a stock investment.

Most prospective purchasers are looking for a better way of life, which will include more comfort and convenience. You should not be influenced by *exactly* everything that the prospect tells you he must have in his home. Simply understand the basic need that prompts his requirement. Try to find and show those homes that most closely fit his emotional needs. There is no perfect home. You have to weigh the benefits and then show the prospect the way.

Create Desire

Some agents feel that they cannot sell a house that they themselves do not like. You don't have to like the home you are selling. *The prospect has to like it.* A sales professional seldom shows his prospects more than three houses, nor does he need to take them out more than one time. The only exception is when he cannot find exactly the right home for them. If he does not have what they are looking for, he admits it, and lets them know he will be searching for it. When such a house is listed, he will immediately phone them to come out to see it. He will, at that time, call and say: "I have just found *your house! Come right out before it gets snapped up. It just won't last. Shall I come by and pick you up now?"*

A sales professional knows how to strengthen the prospect's desire for ownership where only a small interest exists. Some prospects are relatively easy to sell but others are strongly resistant about committing themselves. Once you can overcome the mental obstacles they place in your path, most prospects can be sold. But first it is necessary to create a sufficient desire. A good salesman learns how to take the lead and influence decisions. He is alert to the feelings of his prospects. If he has listened well to their conversations, he knows exactly what they think they want in a house. When the professional agent asks a question, he stops, looks and listens. He stops talking. He looks for visible reactions. He listens to the answer. Using this answer he can increase the prospects' desire by showing them all the benefits and advantages to be derived from ownership of the house for them.

Demonstrate the Benefits as You Go Along

What makes a successful salesman? The successful salesman sells benefits to the buyer. He does not just sell the house, he sells all the benefits that will accrue through home ownership. He manages to make the prospect feel that he, the salesman, is doing him a favor, and that in buying the particular house, the purchaser's life will become more rewarding. The result is the prospect's desire and willingness to act and the signature on the contract offer. No matter what reasons a purchaser may give for buying a house, the real motive for the purchase stems from the basic question. "What will it do for me?" It either gratifies a wish or meets a desire or need. It is the aim of the salesman to find that need and develop it, in order to motivate the prospect enough to close the sale.

Don't Discuss, In Advance, the Properties That You Will Be Showing

Until you arrive at each property, it is a good idea not to discuss it, except possibly to condition the prospective purchasers as to any defects that they will see. If the property is badly in need of repairs, paint, yard work, etc., advise them of this. In certain cases, it may work to your advantage, especially if the home is priced low. If the prospects love a challenge and a bargain, and like to dig in and repair, this may be the house for them. They will soon be telling you that "it wasn't really as bad as I thought."

Plan Your Showing for Maximum Effect

As you drive up to the property, point out the neighborhood features, such as parks, schools, shopping centers, churches, library, recreation, etc. As you near the house, note the trees, lawns and landscaping, if they show well. If the house is in an attractive setting, drive up and park so that the view is unobstructed. When showing the interior, discourage the seller from tagging along. Introduce yourself and your prospects at the door; explain to the seller that you are familiar with this home and know your way around. Be friendly but firm, and smile so that he will take no offense, and he will leave you alone. Buyers turn shy with the seller in attendance and may refrain from asking questions or voicing opinions and objections that you want to eliminate at the source. If the seller does not take your hint, try this: "Mr. Seller, where will you be sitting if we have any questions to ask?"

When showing the interior of the house, if there are stairs leading to upper or lower levels, always show the upper floors first, so that you do not have breathless prospects as you leave. You want their final impression to be one of peace and relaxation. Don't be a "pointer." A rookie agent will sometimes become a pointing robot, saying: "This is the kitchen; this is the bathroom; this is the closet." Showing a house to its best advantage is an art. As you enter with your prospects, prevent the man and woman from going off in different directions. Walk in backwards, if necessary. Say: "Let's go into the living room first." Keep walking, facing them. If you turn around, you may lose them. When you come

"And this is the closet."

to a small room, don't you walk in; it will only make it appear smaller.
If you are in a room with a single window, don't darken the room by
standing in front of the window. Go first directly to those features that
you think will attract them. Walk through the remainder of the house.
Then go back to the first (attractive) part of the house before leaving.
The prospects will be less negative about any faults they may have
found in between. Remember, as you point out the features of the home,
try to emphasize those that you found to be "essential" for this prospect
and tie in the benefits of those features. Some examples are as follows:

- Encourage the prospects to see themselves enjoying all the benefits, comforts and conveniences they would have by owning this
  house, by pausing at the den and saying to the man: "Now here
  is the real living room for the man of the house." Encourage him
  to see himself seated in his easy chair, smoking his favorite pipe,
  with his dog at his side.

- Precede the woman into the kitchen and stand with your back
  to the picture window so that she will have to face it to talk
  with you. While she is looking at the garden, you might say:
  "What a sunny, cheerful kitchen this is, and what a lovely view!"
  If you can get the prospects picturing themselves actually enjoying the benefits of the home and placing their furniture in the
  rooms, you have a good chance of selling them this house.

- "The back yard is completely fenced, so that you can put the
  baby [dog, cat, etc.] there for complete safety and peace of
  mind."

- "This pull-down stairway leads to the attic. What a great place
  to store all those seasonal items." [Christmas decorations, etc.]

- "The laundry room is here, right next to the kitchen. No going
  up and down stairs. And your clothes can be washing while you
  are in the kitchen preparing dinner."

- "The elementary school [if there are small children in the family]
  is right up the street. No waiting in the rain for the bus."

- "Note the level yard. No mountain climbing when you mow this
  lawn."

Get Seller and Buyer to Approve of
Each Other, When Showing Homes

If the seller and prospective purchaser find that they like each other
while you are showing a home, the seller will do everything he can to

make it easy for this particular prospect to buy his home. I have sometimes had difficulty convincing sellers, who were my clients, not to accept
an obviously detrimental contract offer presented by another agent, because they liked the other prospects. They kept saying: "But they're such
a nice couple. I wish they could buy it." When you show prospects
through a home, try to give them a chance to get acquainted, so that,
should you go back and write a contract offer on this house, the sellers
will remember your prospects favorably. However, don't linger if the
prospects have already signalled to you that they do not like the house.

Overcoming Objections Effectively
as You Go Along

Objections should be welcomed as you go along. These show that
your prospect is at least interested in what you are showing. Your responses to these objections should become second nature. When a prospect simply walks through the rooms, making no comments at all, asking
no questions, you know you have no buyer. You also have no buyer if,
when you ask a question it is completely ignored, and when you ask
him if he has any questions, he just says "no."

When the prospect points out a defect or raises an objection, don't
feel that you have to defend the property. *Always agree*, but qualify
this by adding something positive about the house. It is better to face
the objection now than to have it crop up when you are trying to close
the sale. In fact, you should point out the defects yourself, if they are
obvious, so that the prospect realizes that you are on his team.

If the prospect suddenly turns negative, stop everything, and try
to find out what is bothering him. If the woman says: "I don't like the
entire layout of the house" you need to find out what type of floor plan
she is actually seeking, so you ask her: "What do you mean?" Her answer
may give you a clue to the home she is seeking. When you do not find
this out at the beginning, you can be showing all the wrong homes, and
never make the sale. For example, if the woman does not like the entry-
way and says so while you are showing her the house, you can suggest
that the entire effect can easily be changed by just adding a bookcase
near the door, etc. If she says she cannot live without a fireplace, you
can point out a wall which is the ideal place for a custom fireplace with
hearth. However, if the objection is lack of bedrooms, or if the rooms
are too small, or if there are not enough bathrooms, you know that you
have to find a larger house. You cannot suggest that she discard her
children or her furniture. Sometimes, if the price of a home is right, minor
objections can be overlooked, if you can suggest reasonable alternatives.

Getting the Prospect to Look at Homes
Another Day

If a prospective buyer has not bought this day, and you feel that he is a good prospect, you can get him back to look at homes again, with this type of phone call:

Hello, this is Charlotte Korn. I just had to call you. A house has just been listed and it looks exactly like what you are seeking. It has *everything*. And you should see the wallpaper! The price is great! [Put a lot of excitement into your voice.] I know it won't last. Come right out to see it before it gets sold. Shall I come by and pick you up now?

Follow-up Is Important

It is important to follow up on your prospects and keep in touch with them. Remember you already have an investment in them. You may have spent time showing them homes and the right one was unavailable at that time. Or they may have made too low an offer and lost the home they liked. Keep in touch with them and advise them of the new homes as they are listed, and they will not look elsewhere. The second time around this prospect usually acts faster, and it means a quick sale.

I once had a call from a woman who had just signed a year's lease on a home. Even though she had only been renting for one month, she already knew that this was the style of home she wanted. She told me that if I could locate one just like it, in the same elementary school district—one that would be available when her lease was about to expire in about eleven months, she would buy it. About ten months later, one came on the market and I was on the phone within minutes. I arranged to pick her up, showed her the house and she loved it. That night I took her husband out to inspect it. All I needed to do then was write the contract offer; which I did, right on her kitchen table. They bought the house and I earned an easy commission, because of follow-up.

▪ GETTING THE PROSPECT
TO MAKE AN OFFER

Putting It All Together

After you and your prospects have inspected the homes and re-turned to the office, head for the conference room (or wherever you can have some privacy). If there are children tagging along, get them interested in a coloring book, etc. Place a pad of contract offer forms in full view on the table; together with a credit sheet, two pads of paper (one for the prospect) and the mortgage finance books you use. You should also have copies of the listings of homes you have just visited and at least two pens. You don't want *that* excuse for their not signing a contract offer. You should, of course, know which home or homes appealed to the prospects. Review the ones you have visited and refresh their memory by mentioning items on which they commented favorably. (The one with the lovely garden; the one with the gold carpeting and blue appliances, etc.) Concentrate on these items that you know they want in their new home. Then say:

Let's see how it all looks on paper.

And proceed to write. No matter what you write, they will be watching you. *You want their attention.* Then give them a pad of paper and let them "help" you figure out the costs—make them a part of it all. Invite their comments. You can even look up the mortgage rates together. Answer all their questions truthfully and to the best of your knowledge. If you do not know an answer or aren't sure, attempt to find out. Never tell them anything that you are not positive is correct, as this can become the reason for their not buying. You must have their complete trust. Let them discuss the homes they have just visited. Sit back and listen. *Don't leave the room unless it is an emergency* or they ask you to do so. You want to hear what they have to say. This may be their very first home and it is a big decision for them to be making. Be patient. Be sincerely interested in helping them to do the best thing. If you are not sincere, it will show.

Importance of Timing

Timing is extremely important for the close. It is as important to the salesman as it is to the comedian. The professional salesman recognizes this and chooses the correct time to start closing. Trying to close too early, before there is reasonable evidence that a closing technique will work, can make the prospect feel he is being pressured. He will lose confidence in your motives and shy away. On the other hand, if the salesman talks too much, he can bore the prospect and make him suspicious of the value of the homes he was considering. If he has reached a decision, further efforts on your part such as bringing up subjects which will create doubts or objections can be detrimental to the sale.

The professional observes his prospect, watching for signs that the time has come to close. He knows when to stimulate the prospect's desire and does not allow it to cool, because he knows it will be harder work and take additional effort to stimulate it again.

Trial Closes As Professional Tools

When you feel the time has come to ask the prospect to make an offer, you can use any of several effective closing techniques. Making a final decision is a painful and difficult process for many people, because they are afraid of making a mistake that they will later regret. The "by-pass close" breaks this big decision into many little ones. You accomplish this by asking questions such as: "How many bedrooms do you prefer; how many bathrooms; which model of home (colonial, ranch style, Cape Cod, etc.) are you most interested in?" By matching the preferred features to the homes the prospect has seen and liked, you leave him very little alternative but to buy.

You can also send up some "trial balloons" in the form of questions aimed at testing the "buying climate." If you can get a series of "yes" responses, you are in the right atmosphere for closing. (If the responses are negative, just continue and then try again.) You might ask the following:

- Shall we ask for the area rug?
- Could you use the drapes that are in the living room?
- Would you prefer to settle in 30 days?
- Is the master bedroom large enough?

Sometimes the prospect will help you determine when to start the closing process, by saying: "This is exactly the home we were looking for!"

"Friendly Adviser" Technique

Some prospects are so lacking in confidence in their own decisions, that they need someone they can have confidence in and whom they can respect. They need someone to lean on. This is where you become the "friendly adviser." To use this closing technique effectively, you must have already gained the confidence and respect of your prospect. He must feel that you are completely knowledgeable and understand and appreciate his needs and desires. He should be anxious to turn to you as the expert for advice. To be effective using this technique, you must also present negative features, but be very careful about which homes you are negative. The one you select as completely wrong because of its condition, may have appeal to the purchaser because of its price or location. You must convince the prospective purchaser that you are "advising" him rather than "selling" him.

The Weighing Close

If you find that there are minor objections that are impossible to overcome, don't dwell on them; try to keep the prospect's trend of thought away from them. Direct his attention to the features that please him most, and be sure he is thinking of them when you launch into your selected close. When a prospect tells you that he liked many things about a particular house and was even considering it, but feels that he must have a fence (fireplace, different color scheme, etc.), simply give him a pad of paper and a pen. Draw a line down the center of the sheet and have him list all the things he liked about the house he was considering on one side, and what he felt was lacking on the other. He will soon see that the benefits far outweigh the disadvantages; seeing it in writing will help close the sale.

The Urgency Close

The urgency close is one of the most effective methods for closing. If the prospect has been seeking some unusual or special features and he has found them in the property he is considering, bring them to light at this point. If he has been stressing the importance of having his children walk to school, or has wanted a bus nearby so that he could take it to work, or if his wife wanted to be near shopping and the house he is considering has all these features, write it down on your pad and also note other desirable items such as fence or fireplace. Then point out that the number of houses having all these features is limited and sell quickly. If the price is good, he already knows that it will not remain unsold for long but stress it anyway. Explain to him that the safest way to get what he wants is to make an offer now. *After a certain point stop talking.* Remember, the first one who starts talking at this point loses. After he has made his decision to buy, congratulate him to reassure him of the wise step he has taken.

"I Want to Sleep On It!"

Sometimes, as the prospect becomes aware that he is committing himself to the purchase of a house, he panics and may unconsciously start resisting by setting up barriers. He is genuinely afraid of making a wrong decision. At this point, he may begin to introduce objections in order to give himself time to avoid making an immediate decision. He may say: "I want to sleep on it" or "I want to discuss this with my father (uncle, aunt, brother, etc.)." We call this the "Uncle Louis" objection and we hear it all the time. Find the hidden objection. People usually have two reasons for not buying—one that sounds good and the real one. Learn to use the most important word in selling—"*Why?*" If you learn to handle these objections intelligently by probing for the real source of the hesitation, you will be able to overcome their objections. However, always agree with the prospects, as follows: "Good idea! I can see how you feel. I too think it is a big step, and should be given a lot of thought."

Then start probing for the real reason: "What is it that stands in your way? Why do you want to wait? As you know, this house is being offered through the Multiple Listing Service [or being co-oped] and many agents will be showing it. It is such a lovely home and so well priced—the nicest one around, in fact. It just might not be available when you return." If the prospect says that the price is too high, you can say: "If the price were more attractive, would you buy today?" You have brought it out into the open. Now try to get the prospect to make an offer.

Don't Be Afraid to Ask for the Sale!

Many times, the agent is faced with evasions, objections, obscure motivations and plain irrelevancies. Nothing seems to fit into place. The successful salesman never interprets *"no"* as a personal failure, but as a challenge. Never be afraid to ask for the sale. Many salesmen are hesitant to do so and will prolong asking the prospect to buy until the prospect walks out without committing himself. It is your duty to help the prospect come to the right decision. If you cannot assume this responsibility, you not only fail yourself, but your prospect as well. No matter how hard you work, or how effective you may be in displaying your selling expertise and the handling of objections, until you get the signature on the offer, you have not made the sale. The closing actually starts when the prospect walks through the door of your office. Your first objective is to get and keep his attention and interest in order to build towards the sale. If you feel he is "holding back" his true reasons for not buying the home that is right for him, come right out and *ask him why.* Many prospective buyers need the courage to make this very important decision and the confidence and strength of the professional salesman. If the salesman fails them, they may miss buying the very home that was right for them. So *ask for the sale!*

Offering the "Right" Price

A prospect may ask you if you think the seller will accept an offer below the asking price on his home. He may specify an amount and ask that you just "call the owner and ask him." Explain to your prospect that a verbal contract offer is no offer at all. It must be in writing to be legal and binding. If the seller sees a written offer, he knows that the prospect is serious and may sometimes either accept a lesser amount, or counter it with a figure that is lower than his original asking price. The only sure way to find this out is to make a written offer. No matter what price the seller has set as his asking price, he may accept a lower one when he sees the offer because his personal conditions may have changed since he originally put the house on the market for sale. Perhaps he has already found another house, which he stands to lose unless he can sell his own in a hurry. Perhaps he has started to panic about getting this house sold, and is willing to accept an offer that is lower than any- one had thought to make. Or his wife may be a nervous wreck keeping the children in line and the home in showing condition at all hours, and is pressuring him to accept anything. He may find that he can net more from the sale than he had originally thought possible, because of the type of offer being presented.

Some prospective purchasers will ask you to write an offer that is completely unrealistic and far below the market value for the home. They may think the seller is desperate. Even though it is your duty to present and negotiate all offers, the prospect should be discouraged from making this kind of offer, especially if he seriously wants to buy this house, for the following reasons:

- The seller may resent this attempt to "steal his home" and instead of negotiating it by a counteroffer, will just reject it outright.
- Another contract offer might have been written and presented at the same time that his offer is made, and might be accepted (or

countered) if it is a better one, even though it is for less than the asking price. The home then might sell for a price that your prospect would have been happy to pay. Your prospect would have lost the very house he wanted, because of his very low offer.

It is to your purchaser's advantage to make his initial offer as high as he would be willing to go. Then, if his offer is not accepted at that price, he won't feel that he was cheated out of "his house" and possibly blame you.

When a house is being offered for sale under either VA or FHA terms, and your purchaser wants to make an offer, if the appraisal has already been made you can offer that amount or less and hope that the seller will accept the offer. However, if the appraisal has not yet been received, the selling price will automatically be subject to the appraised value. A home may have been listed for $40,000 under VA terms and a full price contract written for $40,000. If the appraisal comes in at $40,000, you have a valid contract. If, however, the amount of the C.R.V. (Certificate of Reasonable Value) is for any amount less than the contract price (e.g., CRV value $39,500) then the purchaser and seller have to renegotiate the contract. Should the seller refuse to lower his price, the purchaser is permitted to pay over the appraisal value, as long as he is made aware of the amount set forth in the appraisal and signs a statement to this effect. If a prospective purchaser feels that the house he wants is worth the asking price of $40,000, and the appraisal has not yet been ordered, have him offer the full price in his contract offer. If he offers less than the asking price, the offer might be rejected. Should the C.R.V. come in for the full selling price of $40,000, that was what he was willing to pay for the house. If it comes in for less, the seller might possibly be willing to renegotiate the price, to the purchaser's advantage.

A prospect may want to make an offer on a house but he says the price is too high. Perhaps he wants to keep his payments low. One way of lowering the monthly mortgage payments is to make a larger down payment on the house. Perhaps he can shop around and get a better interest rate because of the larger down payment, or a longer term to pay off the mortgage, and thereby reduce his monthly payments. Don't forget to point out that the monthly payments are less than they appear, because interest and real estate taxes are deductible from the purchaser's income when paying income taxes. For example, the monthly payment may be $350, which somewhat scares the prospect. But this consists of principal—$50, interest—$200, real estate taxes—$90, and insurance—$10. Since interest and real estate taxes totaling $290 are deductible for purposes of federal and state taxes, there will be a cash savings of over $100 per month if your prospect is in the 35% tax bracket (i.e., if that is the rate he pays on the top portion of his income), or even more than $100, if he is in a higher tax bracket. He does not have to wait for the end of the year to get this tax refund. He may have his employer reduce his withholding (by filling out a proper form) and actually receive $100 more in cash each month, in his paychecks. The frightening $350 monthly payment is thus reduced to $250, which makes it much easier for the prospect to pay. Furthermore, explain that the $50 payment for principal increases his equity in the house he is buying, and will be returned to him when he eventually sells the house. Points paid by the purchaser can also be deducted as interest in the year of sale, if this has been paid to the lender for the use of his money.

Sometimes the purchaser is short of cash for his down payment or settlement costs. You may be able to work out the following:

Under VA ▪ The seller is permitted to pay part of the settlement costs.

Under FHA ▪ The seller is permitted to pay part of the settlement costs.

Conventional Financing ▪ The seller can pay part of the settlement costs, and hold a second trust (subject to the lender's approval).

Assumption Financing ▪ The seller can pay part of the settlement costs, and take back a second trust.

Where a purchaser is short of money ($1,000, more or less), he may be able to borrow it from a relative, on his insurance policy, or from his credit union. An anxious seller will sometimes split the difference with the purchaser, if you are close enough in your negotiations.

▪ **WRITING THE
CONTRACT OFFER**

Working Out the Deal

Many new salesmen, writing their first contract offer, are so elated and excited that they forget to get it signed by the purchasers, or forget to ask for the check. The offer is a legal document. Every agent should know how to write one long before the occasion to do so arises.

The offer can be written anywhere, on the fender of a car or on the kitchen sink of the home you have just finished showing, and it is binding. Don't be afraid to write the offer, even if the circumstances are a little different and unusual. I once wrote a contract offer even though the buyers were only able to see the outside of the house. No key was available. I had previously inspected this house when the family was in the process of moving. The listing company was out of the area and there was no way of getting a key that day. I convinced the prospects that this house was exactly what they wanted, and that once a key was available, it would be sold. We were able to look through the windows and I could describe the interior to them. They liked it, and we wrote the offer "contingent on the purchasers' viewing and approving the interior of the house as soon as a key is made available." I presented the contract offer and picked up the key at the same time. It was accepted by the sellers. The purchasers then inspected the interior of the house, loved it and removed the contingency.

Sometimes a purchaser is ready to make an offer on a house that he likes but has a house that has to be sold before he will have the money required for this purchase. A contingency offer can be written with a time limit set for the sale of this purchaser's home. When you represent the purchaser, you will want to be certain that his house is priced right and is saleable. If the house is listed with another broker, call him. If he is willing to guarantee the sale of your prospect's home at an acceptable price, you may not need a contingency in the offer he is making to purchase. If the home he has to sell is being offered under all terms, it will be easier to consummate a sale.

Usually, in a contract offer which is contingent on purchaser's home being sold (or some other contingency), the seller will insist on a "kickout" clause. (When you represent the seller, you should insist on it.) This clause permits secondary contract offers to be made until the contingency is removed. If a secondary contract offer is acceptable to the seller, then the original purchaser on the primary contract has a specified time (e.g., 72 hours) to remove the contingency. If he does not, the original contract is void ("kicked out") and the seller can accept the secondary contract as primary.

Specify All Items to be Included, in the Contract Offer

It is important that you specifically write into the contract offer all the items that are to be included in the sale of the house. Don't assume because the seller took your prospect aside and told him that the carpeting would be professionally cleaned and he was leaving the lawnmower, that this would be done. The seller may intend to do so, but to make sure that he actually does, write it into the contract offer. Otherwise, he may forget what he promised when he was so desperate to sell. If there is a television antenna on the roof and your purchaser would like this included in the offer, and the seller has in fact told you he was willing to leave it, write it into the contract offer. If the purchaser would like the heating and air conditioning system to pass inspection for a service contract by a service company, write it in. Remember, once the offer is accepted by the sellers, they will reread it completely to see if they are supposed to leave the drapes or freezer and may possibly regret the promises they made, but they know that these items must remain because the contract offer spells it out. If the purchaser noted certain defects in the house while inspecting it (broken window, screen missing, etc.) and would like them corrected by the seller prior to settlement, it should be so noted in the contract offer.

If the contract offer has been written for an assumption of the loan, you might request that the "escrow remain with the loan." This means that the money that the sellers have accrued in their escrow fund with the mortgage lender, would be transferred to the purchaser when he assumes the loan on the house. This, in effect, lowers the net amount the seller receives from the sale of his house. Where the seller is extremely anxious to sell, he may be willing to allow the "escrow to remain with the loan." But specify it in your offer. (Whenever you represent the seller and you present a contract that contains such a clause, make sure that your clients, the sellers, know exactly what it means.)

Escrow Deposit

When a contract offer is written, the prospective buyer must give you a deposit to show the offer is made in earnest ("earnest money"). This is usually in the form of a check, made out to your broker's escrow account. It should be for a substantial sum, the minimum amount being set by your office policy. I always try to get $2,000 and never take less than $1,000 (our office policy). This escrow deposit is written into the contract offer, which is also a receipt for the money. Where the prospective purchaser is not prepared to give you an escrow payment (perhaps his account is being transferred) most REALTORS will take a short-term note to be redeemed within a few days in lieu of a check. When you accept a note, make sure you follow up with your prospect and have him redeem the note on time.

Should the contract offer not be accepted, the escrow deposit is returned to the prospect. Should the contract be accepted, the purchaser gets credit for the escrow deposit at settlement, towards the total price. The escrow deposit serves as a "binder" (sometimes called this) to bind the purchaser to complete the sale. It inhibits second thoughts on the part of the purchaser, once a valid contract has been signed. No one wants to lose $1,000 or $2,000.

Pre-occupancy and Post-occupancy Agreements As Part of the Contract

When a purchaser needs to occupy the house he is buying before settlement can take place, and early occupancy is agreeable to the sellers and the purchasers, it is necessary to write a separate *pre-occupancy* agreement, which spells out the terms of the pre-occupancy. The contract should specify the date of possession and the amount of rent to be charged per day. When a prospective purchaser accepts a pre-occupancy agreement and moves into the premises, it is as though he was moving in after settlement, and he becomes liable for any defects that occur after the 24 or 48 hour period he has in which to report any non-functioning appliances (washer, dryer, dishwasher, etc.).

Where the seller needs to remain on the premises after the house has been sold and settlement has taken place, this should again be covered in the contract, and by separate *post-occupancy* agreement. Under these terms, the seller remains as a tenant, but must maintain the premises in the condition they were in when the house was settled. This type of agreement is generally for the convenience of the seller, whose new home may not have been completed on time. Most purchasers are not willing to permit the seller to remain on the premises after settlement. Sometimes it is the only way to accommodate both sides and complete a contract. Being able to give immediate occupancy, or allowing the seller to remain on after settlement, can be a last minute inducement to clinch the sale. If it is just a question of a day or two either way, this can be adjusted at settlement, with either the purchaser or the seller paying on a per diem basis for the day or two.

Terms of Financing Are Part of the Contract Offer

The listing will specify the types of financing acceptable to the seller—assumption of existing mortgage, VA loan, FHA loan, conventional loan, trade or cash. In many cases, you have a choice of financing methods. Sometimes, by choosing right, you can convert an "iffy" offer into a solid one. It is important to find out before you write the contract offer, the following:

- Who holds the existing mortgage; the current balance; the interest rate and whether the loan is assumable.
- Whether the seller himself would take back a mortgage, and, if so, of what value and at what interest rate.
- Whether the seller would be willing to pay part of the settlement costs normally paid by the purchaser.
- If a VA or FHA appraisal has been ordered and the appraisal value, if it has been set.

A description of the various financing methods and the advantages of each is found in Chapter Four on "Financing." In writing a contract offer, you should be aware of the possible alternatives and see how they fit your prospect's financial requirements. The more familiar you become with the current mortgage market, the greater flexibility you will have in putting deals together.

Closing Costs

The costs for transferring real estate are substantial—very roughly 5% of the price. Your prospective buyer will want to know the amount since he will have to pay it in cash at settlement. With experience, you will be able to estimate these costs fairly accurately. Until you get this experience, consult with your sales manager or one of your experienced associates. Be sure to tell your prospect that the figure is an estimate and subject to change. Most offices have a form that lists the items normally charged to the purchaser, including recording fees and taxes, title charges, origination fee (points), appraisal fee, credit report charge, etc.

Beware of the
"Time is of the Essence" Clause

Never insert the phrase "time is of the essence" in a contract offer, and if you are presented with an offer that has this phrase, protect your client by having it removed. Real estate contracts are usually written with approximate dates and time periods—for example: "settlement in 60-90 days"; or "on or about September 1st." Experienced agents appreciate the reason for this. There are many unforeseen events—delays in paperwork, etc., that may happen between the acceptance of the contract offer and final settlement, and it is impossible to guarantee a particular date or time period when writing the contract. If you insert "time is of the essence" into the contract, you are giving that guarantee and may kill your deal if settlement is delayed even slightly. Should your prospect or client require settlement by a specified day, promise him you will do your best to expedite (and do it), or possibly work out his problem some other way (by pre-occupancy, post-occupancy, or the advancement of money, etc.).

I learned all about "time is of the essence" the hard way. A contract offer was delivered to me on a house that I had listed. It contained the phrase "settlement by June 1st. Time is of the essence." Since this date was four months away, I thought there could not possibly be any problems and accepted it. The contract offer was accepted by the sellers and the purchaser immediately made loan application. He was in for a big surprise. The interest rates had suddenly sky-rocketed. He started to shop around for a lender who would give him better terms. The terms offered were no better. By the time he was able to find and accept the terms offered by a lender, June 1st had arrived. The seller refused to go through with the contract and the deal was off.

Writing a Contract Offer for a Condominium Unit

As previously indicated, apartments or other residential units which are owned as condominiums may be transferred in the same manner as individual residential homes. But the sale is for the unit itself, plus the pro rata share of the external amenities, such as hallways, lawns, and recreational facilities (together with the obligation to pay a pro rata share of the cost for their maintenance).

The following clause should be added to the contract to cover this point. The condominium sale can then be handled in the same way as any other sale:

> Purchaser agrees to abide by the condominium rules and to use and to occupy the condominium premises subject and subordinate in all respects to the provisions of the Master Deed and the By-laws and Rules and Regulations relating to the use of the common elements, or other "House Rules" of the Association.

The Condominium Association may have its own required clause to be inserted into any contract written for the sale of any of their units. Check with them.

When Purchaser or Seller is a
Real Estate Agent

Sometimes you, the real estate agent, will be selling your own home, or perhaps you will be in the market to buy one for your own use, or as an investment. In order to protect yourself from possible lawsuits, you should insert a clause into the contract, stating the fact that you are an agent, as follows:

Seller is advised that purchaser is a real estate agent employed by
._____ Company, and agrees to indemnify _____
Company and said agent from any and all claims of conflicts of interest.

Be a Good Sport if You Don't
Make the Sale

When you realize that this is not your day to sell, and that all attempts you have made to close were resisted, you can only thank the prospects for coming in, give them any house literature you have, together with your card, and ask that when they call again to make sure to ask for you by name; then *let them go.* Assure them that you will contact them immediately if the exact house they are seeking gets listed. Then ask yourself:

- Did I listen and try to find out what the prospect's needs were?
- Did I counter objections effectively?
- Did I have product knowledge?
- Did I have the proper degree of enthusiasm?

A willingness to examine your failures, identify them and then do something about them, is the key to success. No one is perfect and we all make mistakes. A close objective look at your own errors can help you on the way to success.

If you are not a good sport and tend to become angry with the prospect, you will defeat your main purpose which is to make future sales. Your prospect will reflect your mood and when you phone him again, he will act cold. On the other hand, if you maintain your friendliness in spite of his reluctance to buy on this day, he will remember you favorably. Make sure you enter his name on your follow-up calendar.

Also be sure to put his name and phone number in the office log book, in case he phones in some day and forgets your name. Even if he calls you to say that he has found his new home in another area, be a good sport! His deal may not go through. In any case, you may receive future referrals from this prospect because of your cooperative attitude. Don't get discouraged. You can't win them all. I have always felt that if you throw enough against the wall, some of it has to stick. So keep in there pitching!

chapter six

AFTER YOU HAVE
THE CONTRACT OFFER

▪ PRESENTING
THE OFFER

Prepare for the Presentation

Presenting a contract offer is a highly skilled job. It involves much more than handing the papers to the seller and saying: "Here is a contract offer on your house." It requires careful preparation and skillful negotiating. A house is not "sold" until the purchaser's offer has been accepted and signed by the sellers.

You can never predict what will happen at a presentation even if the offer is for the full price. I once wrote an excellent, full-priced contract offer on a house listed by another agent and we both went to present the offer that evening about 9 P.M. The woman (seller) let us in, but took us aside to explain that her husband had just come home from a party and was slightly inebriated. She was putting it mildly. He was *stoned*. She put up a large pot of coffee and then fed him cup after cup, trying to revive him. By 11:30 that night, he was gradually becoming aware of his surroundings and noticed us. By midnight, he started to feel things and we were able to present the offer, which was gladly accepted and signed by both husband and wife. We all sighed with relief as the other agent and I took our leave. We had, however, caught up with all of our favorite evening programs on TV that night.

When a contract offer on your listing is written by another agent, he may want to go along when you present his offer. This is standard procedure in our area. The offer should be presented as soon after it is received as is possible. (If more than one contract offer is written, both are presented at the same time.) When you set up the presentation appointment, be sure both husband and wife will be home, and set the appointment for after dinner, when the children are out of the way. Unless it is an offer for the full asking price, have someone else make the appointment call for you. Reason? Since the seller is anxious to

know how much is being offered, that will be his first question when
he hears your voice on the phone. You may have to tell him the price
and therefore stand a good chance of an immediate rejection. The seller
might say: "Don't even bother to come out. That man wants to steal my
house!" Avoid this situation by having a co-worker call to set up the appointment for you. If the seller should ask about the price, your co-
worker can honestly say he doesn't know. If you find you must make
the call yourself, avoid getting into a position where your client can
make his decision over the phone. If I am pressed for price, I say: "I
haven't had a chance to review it yet—I'm on my way over right now."

When the offer is for less than the listed price, don't try to prejudge
what the seller's decision will be. What you may think is an unacceptable
offer, may be "just dandy" to the seller, who may be more anxious than
you realize to sign and accept. However, to increase the likelihood of
acceptance, there are several steps necessary before you set up the presentation appointment:

1 ■ Review the sellers' file so that you know the terms and conditions of the listing agreement and can talk intelligently about
the property. If it was priced above the market value, in spite
of the fact that you had recommended a lower asking price
($45,000 instead of $43,000 as you suggested), and if the only
two offers received in the past three months were for $41,500
and $42,000, you will want to point this out to the sellers,
should they feel that they are being offered less than their
home is worth.

2 ■ Have the sellers already located a new home? When do they
have to settle on it? Do they need the proceeds of this sale in
order to do so?

3 ■ Examine the contract offer. Then have your sales manager go
over it carefully. If it has any clauses you do not understand,
or contingencies that may prove objectionable, you will want
to be ready with your answers, explanations and suggestions.
Review it as to price, terms and requested occupancy. How
do these compare with the sellers' requirements?

4 ■ Review the buyers' credit sheet. Do they have a house to sell?
How will their credit look to the finance company? Do they
have the required cash for the down payment and closing
costs? Where are they from? How many children do they
have? When must they have possession?

5 ■ Check comparables (similar homes sold) that have come on
the market since this one was listed. What were the asking

prices? How long were they on the market before being sold? At what prices were they finally sold and under which terms and conditions?

Project Confidence

An agent who has kept in touch with the sellers he represents, who has advised them of the progress and activity, the advertising and comments by prospective purchasers and other agents, can expect to have good rapport with them, and should not be fearful of presenting a contract offer no matter what the price. Never be apologetic. Walk in with assurance. You have accomplished what you set out to do and have had action on the sale of their home. Even though the offer is not for the full asking price, you have still exposed their house to other agents and other real estate companies, and you arranged for it to be further exposed by advertising. You have kept in touch with them to advise them of your progress and here is the written proof of your efforts—an offer to buy. You will present it fairly and they will have the option of either accepting it, rejecting it, or making a counteroffer.

Explain the Contract

Upon arriving for the presentation appointment, exchange some friendly greetings and select the room with the most conducive setting to discuss the offer. My preference is the kitchen, with its large table and good lighting. I dislike the living room, where you have to either sit between husband and wife, or where you are seated across the room, with a small, cluttered coffee table in between. If a TV set or radio is on, ask if they would have any objections to turning it off. They generally do not. Sit facing both husband and wife so that you can talk to both at the same time and neither one feels neglected. Spend a few minutes on small talk. (How is their other house progressing?) You can tell them that the buyers just loved their house, and they may then comment that they thought that the "nice couple had such a well-behaved little girl." You can volunteer where the purchasers are from. If they feel warmly towards the purchasers, they may be more flexible in their attitude about price and conditions. If more than one contract offer is being presented at this time, advise the sellers that *they* will be making the final decision, based on a full disclosure of all information written in each. It is your duty to fairly advise the sellers of the merits of each offer.

Separate the contract offer copies; give one to the husband and another to his wife, so that each one can follow you as you read and explain the offer. If it is a good offer despite the fact that it is not for the full asking price, you can tell them so. Explain that even though an offer is made for less than the asking price, it may still net them more cash than they had anticipated. For example, if the house was offered under all terms, the seller would have had to pay points under a VA or FHA offer. Since this contract offer is for an assumption of the loan, and there are no points involved, the seller will be saving a substantial sum.

"How Much Will I Net?"

This question, of course, is the most important one that the sellers will ask. They will be waiting patiently for you to come to this part of the presentation. Explain exactly how much they should clear, after commission, mortgage pay-off, pre-payment penalties (if any), legal expenses and other selling costs. Don't forget that some assumption loans carry charges when the loan is assumed. Be sure to explain each point clearly so that *they understand you.* I write the figures as I quote them directly on my folder where they become a permanent record, should the sellers later "recall" they were promised a larger net return. If the sellers have an escrow fund, advise them that this will be added to the amount that they will receive when the house finally settles.

Be sure to remind the sellers that the profit (capital gain) on the sale of their house is not taxable if they buy another home of equal or better value within 18 months. Persons 65 years of age or older will have all or a major portion of the profit, tax free, providing this was their principal residence for at least 5 of the last 8 years. Furthermore, the apparent profit on the sale can be reduced by deducting the expenses that were shown on the closing statement when the house was originally purchased, such as survey, appraisal fee, title insurance, etc.; any expense incurred to improve the property within 90 days before the contract date may also be deducted from the gain. If there has been a fee paid in order to obtain the loan (points), or other charges, they, too, are deductible. However, all these comments on taxes should be checked against current regulations, as they do change.

Sometimes an assumption contract offer contains the following clause: "Escrow to remain with the loan." The first time I saw this clause on a contract offer, I didn't understand what it meant. An offer had been delivered to me on a house I had listed. It looked like a good one and was for the full asking price for assumption of the loan, except for the above clause. My sales manager explained that the term meant that the purchaser was asking for any escrow balance that had accrued (generally taxes held by the mortgage company for future payment of taxes) and which belonged to the seller. This was unusual in our selling area, so we rejected that item in our counteroffer. (I later found that it was quite common to request that the escrow remain, in other areas of the country.)

Note that once a contract is accepted and signed, the sellers cannot remove any items listed in the contract, or any items described in the VA or FHA appraisal as being part of the appraised value. If the seller removes an old washer or refrigerator, he will have to replace it, at possible additional cost. Make sure he understands this.

Avoid Making Minor Changes in the Contract Offer

If the price and the terms of the contract offer are generally acceptable, warn your seller that if he changes it in any way, it constitutes a counteroffer. This permits the prospective purchaser not only to accept or reject the countered item, but to reject the entire contract. This is quite risky, because the prospect may have had second thoughts about buying, and now he can get his escrow deposit returned.

When I was a rookie, I once let my seller change the settlement date from 40 days to 45 days. (He insisted he might need more time to find a place.) That night, when the prospective buyer was asked to initial the change, he decided that he preferred a different model house, rejected the counteroffer, and I lost a sale. Another time, a seller insisted that I insert a clause into the contract offer stating that his antenna would not remain. I pointed out to him that any change constituted a counteroffer and also that the purchasers did not even want the antenna. They had a rotor one for color. However, he insisted that the clause be inserted. The first thing the prospective purchasers asked me was: "What happens if we do not initial the change." I had to tell them. Again, they had changed their thinking and decided to wait a few months before making a decision, and I lost the sale.

Contingent Contracts

It is your duty as a real estate salesman to protect the sellers whom you are representing. That is why they called and asked for *you* in the first place. If the contract offer contains a contingency clause, *read it carefully*. Should it be "contingent on the sale of the purchaser's home" in another part of town, the sellers should be made aware of this, and understand that should the purchaser not sell his home, their contract

will be void, and the house will have to be put back on the market for
another offer.

   If the contingency is that a parent (who will be coming into town
in a week) will have to approve the purchase, it will mean taking their
house off the market for a week. Remember, the parent may or may not
approve the purchase. Where the sellers are in no great hurry and the
contract offer containing a contingency is highly acceptable in every
other way, your clients may choose to accept it. You can, however, limit
the time that it will be off the market by countering with a kick-out
clause, wherein the purchasers have a specified number of days to remove
the contingency. Or you can add that the "sellers' home is to remain on
the market for secondary contracts." Should one be brought in, then the
purchasers of the primary contract have a given time (e.g., 72 hours) to
remove the contingency, or the secondary contract will become the
primary one.

How to Work With the Low Offer

   You receive an offer on a house you have listed and it is for less
than the seller wanted. However, the seller is concerned about leaving
his family behind with an unsold house, when he must leave for his
new job out of town in a few weeks. The purchasers are very agreeable
and cooperative about all the other conditions of the contract and are
willing to settle and take possession at the convenience of the sellers.
All of these factors often sway the sellers into accepting the offer,
although it is for less money.

   When the offer you are presenting is exceptionally low, you should
explain to the seller that you did not set this price—that the purchasers
did. You are required by law to present all written offers, and you are
doing so. If the seller's immediate reaction is one of anger, don't show
him that it upsets you. Just wait for him to simmer down, and then explain that he has alternatives. He can accept the offer (obviously he is
not about to accept this one!), he can reject it, or he can negotiate it.
Remind the seller that, although the offer is low, it is still a legitimate
one, and the purchasers have put down a substantial deposit in making
their offer. Let husband and wife discuss between themselves the merits
of the offer. He may choose to do some arithmetic and look through his
papers. Just busy yourself with your file. If they say they would like
to hold it overnight and not make an immediate decision—possibly that
nice couple who were just here might make a better offer—remind them
that many people have already been to the house, but made no offers;
that this is a bona fide offer, even though it is low, which has possibili-

ties; that the purchasers may go home and wonder if their bid was too high, or may think that perhaps a better value might come on the market if they wait for a few days.

Show the sellers what the comparable homes have been selling for and recommend that they counter the contract rather than reject the offer. You might still work it out. Explain that once the house is actually sold, they can relax. No more people coming through at all hours. Hand them your pen and show them where to sign!

Avoid Yo-Yo Negotiations

You may have a very low offer to present to your clients, the sellers, which was made by a prospective buyer who expects to counter back and forth, like a yo-yo. Explain to your sellers that this may possibly be such a prospective buyer. Recommend that rather than reject the contract offer, they decide in their own minds the very lowest price they will accept, and counter at this price. If they agree, make the necessary changes in the counteroffer, have them sign and initial the changes, but add a time limit for the counteroffer to be accepted or rejected by the prospective purchaser. Then explain to the agent representing the prospective buyer that this is the rock bottom price acceptable to the sellers; he should advise his buyer to accept or reject only.

When the Sellers Are Out of Town

Sometimes the sellers are away for a week or two, and a contract offer is brought in. Perhaps the husband has already started on his new job, and it is impossible for him to return at this time. The family may have already moved to their new home in another state before the house was sold. You should, of course, have a forwarding address and phone number for just such a contingency. Call the sellers and present the contract offer by phone, exactly as you would in their home. If they accept verbally, great. Have them wire their acceptance directly to your office, and ask them to request Western Union to phone it in, and then mail the telegram to your office, to your personal attention. Should they decided to counter the offer, or reject it, have the telegram specify the terms that they are now giving to you verbally. The telegram should state, in effect:

We accept contract dated _____ by Mr. and Mrs. _____ for purchase of our home at _____ under _____ (VA, FHA, Conv., Assumption, etc.) terms, for $_____ with $_____ down.

This should be signed in both names, and is a legal acceptance of the offer until the original contract can be mailed to them for their signatures.

■ AFTER THE CONTRACT OFFER IS ACCEPTED

"Congratulations: You Have Just Bought a House!"

When you finally say these words to the purchasers, don't rush right out to spend your commission! Not for a long while yet. From the time the contract offer is signed by the prospective purchasers and presented to the sellers for their acceptance and possible counter, to the time that you go to settlement and all sit facing the settlement attorney, a lot has to happen. You probably will be showing the house to the purchasers again and again because they "really didn't see it in full daylight," and then they will have to bring their parents out and later a favorite uncle. Another time the purchasers will be calling to ask if they can come out to measure the windows, floors, etc. Of course there is also the appraiser, the termite inspector and the purchasers again to take one last look. On the day of settlement, they may want a pre-settlement inspection of the house and will get you up bright and early to have enough time to see if the washer and dryer are working, and they will meet you at the house with a week's supply of laundry. But it is finally settling—*hurrah!*

Although you have a signed and accepted contract, things can still happen to the deal. One of our agents wrote a contract offer on a house and the prospect filled out a credit sheet. Everything looked ideal. The man looked like a high school principal and his wife looked like a business woman. They loved everything about the house and immediately set up an appointment to make a loan application. The selling agent walked around on "cloud 9" since he had sold one of the higher priced homes and his commission would be substantial. Five days later his bubble burst and he came down to earth with a bang. The credit report was delivered. It was three pages long—all debts! The loan officer confided that this was one of the worst credit reports he had ever seen.

The sellers should be advised that although they have a signed contract of sale, their house is not actually sold until after settlement and recordation and that many problems may arise. Should the interest rate change, this may affect the points they will have to pay. The agent should also prepare his clients for possible delays. Although the VA appraiser has 3 to 10 days in which to come out to appraise their home, and his report should be turned in within two weeks from the date of receipt of the request for appraisal by the Veteran's Administration, he may be late turning it in due to circumstances beyond his control (holidays, illness, etc.). Sellers may read their contract which spells out "60 days from time of acceptance" as the actual settlement date. If they read further, they will see that it continues "or as soon thereafter as a report of title can be secured . . ." Should there be any delay (confirmation of purchaser's bank account, verification of salary, etc.) it will take longer. Also, the case can be held up because of additional requests for information or signatures. A verification of employment form may sit on a vacationing employer's desk or just get lost in the shuffle, and the salesman will find himself hand carrying signed papers in order to keep his case moving. But there is only so much the agent can do. Some lenders make their requests for additional information one item at a time. Each time the agent thinks the case is ready for settlement and requests a date, he finds that there is still another form which is missing or in need of signatures. *Only after the purchaser has been approved for the loan should the sellers start making their moving plans.* So although the sellers may be counting the days, lenders have many cases to process and cannot be pushed. VA and FHA cases average a certain length of time to process and a case may come out of VA and instead of an approval, you find it contains a request for additional information, which necessitates more delay.

A contract that is contingent on the sale of the purchaser's home may become invalid if the purchaser has overestimated the value of his home and then it appraises for far less, making it impossible for him to come up with the necessary cash for his purchase. I once presented a full-priced VA contract offer on a house that was already VA appraised, only to later learn that the purchaser was not a veteran and his agent had been unaware of this fact when the contract offer was written.

Applying for the Loan

After the contract offer is accepted by the seller, it is necessary for the purchaser to make loan application with a lender (unless the house is being sold on an assumption basis and it may not be required, or on a cash basis). In some real estate offices, this is arranged by their processing department. In others, the individual agent sets up the appointment with the lending institute. The purchaser takes with him the following:

1 ▪ A copy of the contract of sale.
2 ▪ The account numbers and current balances for all his checking, savings and credit union accounts.

3 ■ The account numbers for any recurring debts he may have such as bank notes, installment loans, personal loans, revolving charge accounts, etc.

4 ■ Information with reference to his employment and his wife's, if she is working. This would include copies of W-2 forms for the past two years (complete tax returns if the purchaser is self-employed).

5 ■ Credit processing fee.

If it is necessary for the loan officer to order a VA or an FHA appraisal, the following will also be required:

1 ■ Fee for VA or FHA appraisal.

2 ■ On VA loans—Certificate of Eligibility, or the veteran's form DD 214 (separation papers from the service) in order to obtain the certificate.

3 ■ Complete property description (generally a copy of the listing serves this purpose).

4 ■ House location survey (plat). Also, directions to the property from a main highway, plus owner's name, phone number and present address.

Processing the Case

Many real estate companies have a processing department to follow up on the case from here. However, the salesman should follow up on the processing department. The salesman should be sure that he turns over to the processing department all the necessary documents, including the signed contract, escrow check, credit sheet and any other forms his office requires. Also any phone numbers where the sellers can be reached if they have already moved, together with the new address. This omission on his part might result in long delay.

In a VA or FHA sale, where an appraisal is being ordered, make sure you note in your diary when *you think* the appraiser should be out to inspect the house. (I leave instructions with the sellers to call me when the appraiser calls them to set up this appointment.) After the appraiser has been out to the house, mark the date in your diary when you think the appraisal is due back. You don't want your case to get lost in any shuffle! Remember, until the appraisal is in, you do not have a firm contract under VA or FHA terms.

When a house is sold under conventional terms, it is much simpler. You will want to know when the appraiser has been out to inspect the property, if the purchaser's necessary verifications are in (employment, bank, etc.) and if the termite inspection has been made. Again, I make all these notations directly onto the folder so that there is no searching or trying to remember dates. Remind the purchaser that he will need an insurance policy for settlement. Work out a settlement time mutually acceptable to buyer, seller and attorney, after the case is completed, and then make sure you are available on that day. Along the way, always keep in touch with the seller or the buyer (or both, if you represent them both) so that they do not feel abandoned. Also check up on their actions. I once routinely called the purchaser I was representing (a young man who was buying a house under conventional terms, with $6,000 down) only to learn that he was on his way out to buy a $6,000 car, and in so doing, would be removing all of his funds from the bank. I quickly explained the facts of life to him, and he cancelled the order for the car.

If you represent the seller, be sure to tell him not to order the utilities turned off on settlement day, but to have them transferred to the new owner's name as of that date. If you represent the buyer, you advise him to phone the utility companies and have them transferred to his name as of the settlement date. (I know of cases where water pipes froze up because the gas heat was turned off. When the new owner moved into the house a few weeks later and had the heat turned on, the pipes burst.) Also, tell the sellers not to cancel the fire insurance policy on their house until the attorney notifies them that the settlement papers are filed. Should there be a fire during those days before filing, you would not want there to be any question of the insurance coverage.

Don't Forget That Forwarding Address

Getting the forwarding address is extremely important. As a matter of fact, get any addresses and phone numbers you can, when you list a house, especially if the family will be away frequently, looking for another house in another area. If there is a relative nearby, take down that phone number. Get the man's present work number, knowing that his office will probably be able to reach him, should he suddenly move without notifying your office. I once had a last minute change of settlement time, and the sellers' phone had already been disconnected. I drove by and found that they had moved out. Neighbors told me that they

Night before your first settlement.

were staying in a motel until after settlement but didn't know where. The man's office was able to tell me the name of the motel. I called them there, and saved them an unnecessary trip.

One salesman I know listed a house, and a contract offer was brought into the office some time later. This agent tried to call the sellers to present the offer to them, but their phone was disconnected. They had moved and left no forwarding address. He was finally able to track them down, but by that time, the offer had been withdrawn and the house re-listed with another real estate office, where it was promptly sold. It is important that you *get that forwarding address!*

The Settlement

I had been working for only a short time when I persuaded a home-owner who had been advertising his home "For Sale by Owner" to allow me to list it. The following week, I sold this house to a young couple who had just dragged themselves into our office. It was a dreary, rainy night. They had a sleeping baby in the back seat of the car and had been driving all day. *My first listing and my first sale!*

The day of settlement dawned. Being new in the business and never having attended a settlement, I tried to find out just what one did there. All my associates were as "green" as I was, and could offer no help at all. My sales manager, however, had his own peculiar brand of humor, and I could not get a straight answer from him. The conversation went as follows:

Me: What do I do at a settlement?

S.M.: You just sit between the buyers and the sellers.

Me: But I must have some function. What do I do?

S.M.: You just keep them from fighting.

Me: Fighting??? What do they have to fight about?

S.M.: There you go again—anticipating trouble.

Me: I just want to be prepared. This is my first settlement. What can they possibly want to fight about?

S.M.: You never know till it comes up!

You can imagine with what uneasiness I left for this ordeal. Actually, it all went very smoothly.

I have since learned to sit with a folder in my lap, pen in hand, knowing look on my face, and periodically leaf through the papers in the file. The attorney does it all. The phone is nearby should anything need clarifying. If you have prepared both buyers and sellers about what they may expect, there should be no surprises at the settlement table. If you represent the sellers, you have already advised them to have the final readings made on the utilities in the house they are leaving, and have recorded their forwarding address on your file. You have told them that there may be a water escrow held by the settlement attorney until the final bill is paid (an unpaid water bill becomes a lien on the property), and how much money they should be expecting from the sale of their home. You also have advised them that the funds may or may not be disbursed the same day. (Some attorneys will not disburse funds until all papers are recorded.)

If you represent the purchasers, you have advised them how much money they will need for settlement and have suggested a certified or bank check. You have reminded them about getting an insurance policy and calling to have the utilities transferred into their account. (I call the utility companies for out-of-town buyers or sellers.) I always tell the buyer it may cost a little more when I estimate his settlement costs, and the seller that he will net a little less. I find that when settlement is over, everybody walks away happy and smiling, including me. I try to attend all of my settlements whether I represent the buyers or the sellers because this creates better future relations. They feel you are interested enough to stay with them through the entire procedure, and they feel more secure.

Many settlement attorneys wait for the last minute to prepare their papers. Often a secretary works up the original figures. The attorney then reviews them for the first time while going over the costs with the buyers and sellers at the settlement table. Sometimes final pay-off figures from the current lender are not available until the morning of settlement and the drafted closing statement must be changed. The agent should check the settlement sheet for possible errors or omissions, particularly where figures have been transferred from one sheet to another. Attorneys and their secretaries are human and mistakes can be made. Familiarize yourself with the settlement sheet.

An experienced agent comes prepared with certain information in order to avoid any possible delay in settlement:

- He knows in advance what the taxes are on the property being sold. Have they been paid? Are they in arrears? Is there a late penalty and how much is being charged? He has these figures with him at settlement. (I went to a settlement recently where the secretary was new and had neglected to find out if the taxes had been paid. Fortunately I could supply this information.)

- Has the termite inspection been made? Has the necessary certificate been forwarded to the attorney's office? Have the purchasers received their insurance policy? Remind them to bring it to settlement.

- Has your client, the seller, at any time placed an additional mortgage on the house? Has he paid off any note or mortgage before settlement? Many sellers will pay off their mortgage and not bother to have this information recorded. They do not know that if this is not put on record, it shows up as unpaid and is a lien on the property. A settlement can be held up until a paid note or mortgage is located.

- Has there been a pre-occupancy of the premises on the part of the purchasers, or a post-occupancy by the sellers? Is there any adjustment of rent required?

- Are there any heating or air-conditioning service contracts that the purchaser may wish to assume and that require a money adjustment?

- Is there a swimming pool membership that is being assigned from seller to purchaser? Any money adjustment? It is surprising how many times a piece of missing information can hold up settlement.

At some point, the attorney will explain Owner's Title Insurance to the buyer and ask whether or not he wishes to purchase it. Title insurance is a special form of insurance which protects against legal flaws in previous ownership. Even though the title search shows no defect on record, there are matters that may not have been recorded—for example, undisclosed heirs, forged signatures or simply errors in recording. If they were to be revealed after the buyer takes possession, they could become a cloud on the title and he would have a difficult time removing it when he wished to sell the property. The lender always protects its equity by obtaining title insurance (called Mortgage Title Insurance) and the premium charge is added to the buyer's settlement costs. The home buyer is offered title insurance to protect his own equity. There is a one-time premium which is added to the buyer's settlement charges if he wants to take the policy and it protects him and his heirs as long as they have any interest in the property.

If you represent the buyer, he may turn to you and ask "Should I take it?" I explain it is really up to him to decide. If he insists on my opinion, I will say that this is a nominal premium cost to pay for peace of mind and will be a small part of his total settlement costs. Should it ever be needed, the buyer will be protected.

When I first started attending settlements where I represented the purchasers, I used to feel uncomfortable. I wondered if I had done the best that I could for them—what was I letting them in for, binding them to house payments for the next thirty years! Months later, I met some of these original buyers and they all thanked me profusely for helping them make the best move of their lives. They were all delighted with their homes, and kept telling me how much their property had appreciated in that short period of time. It put the whole thing into perspective for me.

Actually, for a young couple, it is an excellent step to buy a home. Many who can still buy homes today may not be able to afford them in five or ten years, because of increasing building costs and inflation of home prices.

The Follow-up Book—Your Future Referrals

There is a veritable "gold mine" in future referrals, by following up on your satisfied purchasers and sellers. I have discovered a system that works very well for me, and I know that it will work for you too.

I inherited a 6" x 8" three ring looseleaf book, and it turned out to be exactly the right size for my purpose. I have it arranged with an alphabetic index, and pages can be inserted and removed at will. After settlement, and before I put the file away as closed, I start a page on the purchaser or the seller, whomever I represented in the transaction. If it is the purchaser, I enter the full name of the man and his wife, the address of the home just purchased, and the date of settlement. I note the number of children, the man's employment and his office phone number. If the woman is also employed, I record her number. When their phone is installed at home, I will enter that also. I make a notation in my diary to phone them in about a week. This looseleaf page becomes my permanent follow-up record on the family.

If I have represented the seller, I enter the names of both husband and wife and their forwarding address and phone number, if it is available. Should they later refer any clients or prospects to me, I will want to know where I can write to thank them.

After the purchasers have settled in, I make the first of my many future phone calls to them, wishing them good luck, and asking how they are getting along. From then on, whenever I phone or send a greeting card, I will enter the date of the call on their page, and mark it either "friendly call," "Christmas card" or "New Year's card." When I call, if the woman tells me a child is sick, etc., I note it on the page, and make a notation in my diary to call in a few days. When I do call and ask her how her child is feeling, she is delighted that I have remembered and was thoughtful enough to call. If she tells me she is going on vacation in a few days, I ask her when she will be returning, and note the date in my diary as a reminder to call when she returns. She will be delighted and surprised when I do call her later on and ask her about her trip. We have now become friends. When one of my "satisfied customers" calls me on the phone I have this book handy, and while she is identifying herself, I have already opened to her page and am asking her about her family. I can remember it all with the help of my trusty book, and we chat like old friends. Even though I need my book to jog my poor memory, I am sincerely interested in my clients' welfare, and my conversation reflects this.

There are dividends from these "friendly chats." Sometimes, just before we hang up, the client might say: "We have some friends who are thinking of relocating in this area. Do you think you can find as lovely a home for them as you did for us?" Or she may say: "Do you know the Smiths? I believe they are going to be leaving this area soon. I must tell her to call you to help sell their home." Or—"I have been telling everyone about how helpful you have been in the sale of our home, and how interested you are in the people you work with. I told them to be sure to ask for you by name when they buy or sell their homes." I know that this family will call on me when they are ready to make a change!

chapter seven

YOU ARE IN BUSINESS
FOR YOURSELF

▪ FINANCIAL
BENEFITS

As a real estate salesman you are an independent agent and, for income tax purposes, are considered to be in business for yourself. You should keep accurate records of all your expenses, since you are taxed on the *difference* between your income (commissions) and your business expenses. If you have a room set aside as an office at home, you may pro rate part of your home expenses for business use; similarly, if you use your home telephone. The use of your car for business is usually a major expense. Any out-of-pocket expenses for advertising novelties, such as pens, key holders or calendars, or supplies and postage, would be deductible expenses. Be sure to keep adequate records of any lunches or dinners, or entertaining you do with clients and prospects. If one of your children helps you with errands, putting up signs, or with your paperwork, you can reimburse him for his work; this would be an expense for you. (It would be income for the child, but at his tax rate.)

You may also set aside 15% of your income (up to $7,500) for each year, without paying current income taxes on it, into a retirement fund for yourself, under a Keogh (pronounced "key-ho") plan. If your total family income, including your commissions and your spouse's income, exceeds $20,000, you should definitely get advice from a tax accountant, preferably one with real estate experience. He will advise you of the latest tax benefits, as they change very often. Don't forget that his fee is also a deductible expense.

Simple Bookkeeping

New salesmen (and many oldtimers too) continually ask me how I make sure that all commissions earned are actually paid. Soon after I started selling, I devised a simple recordkeeping system which tells me

SALES RECORD

Date	Seller	Buyer	Address of Property	Lister	Seller	How Sold	Selling Price	Comm. Due	Settl. Date	Commissions			
										Date Paid	Amount	Remarks	
2/3	Smith	Jones	5100 Flower Rd.	Korn	Harvey	VA	30,000	450	3/30	4/5	450		
2/11	Bland	Kane	1260 Gerard St	Davis	Korn/Tuck	Conv.	33,250	250	3/28	4/5	250	Split Comm.	
2/15	Blake	Lewis	3450 Hemp St.	Korn	Roland	FHA	54,000	810					
2/24	Harris	Blake	4400 Harwood Av.	Ketzl	Korn	VA	47,000	705					
3/10	Clay	Williams	2600 Andover Ct.	Korn	Youmans	Rental	400/mo.	50		4/5	50		

COMMISSIONS RECEIVED RECORD

Date of Comm. Check	Amount Received	How Applied	
4/5	$750.00	Smith/Jones	$450.00
		Williams Rental	50.00
		Bland/Kane	250.00
			750.00

all I need to know. I am often amazed at the number of agents who make remarks such as: "I am not sure if I was paid on the Jones sale yet." I can tell at a glance which sales I have been paid for or how much is still due me.

I have two records—a Sales Record and a Commissions Received Record. (See illustrations.) As soon as a contract offer is accepted on any sale where I am the lister or the selling agent, I enter it on the next line of my Sales Record, showing the date of sale, the name of the seller and buyer, the address of property, the listing and selling agents (if the other agent is not with my own company, I write the name of his company as well), how sold (i.e., VA, FHA, Conventional, Assumption), the selling price and the commission due me based on this price. If the selling price is later changed (e.g., as a result of renegotiation after a VA appraisal), I change this record and the amount of commission due accordingly. I enter all rentals in a similar fashion, writing "Rental" in the "How Sold" column and leaving blank any column that does not apply to rentals.

When the case settles, I enter the settlement date which indicates to me that a commission check is expected. When I receive a commission check, I enter it both in my Commissions Received Record and in my Sales Record. That's it. By glancing down the Commissions Due column, I can tell at a glance the total amount still due me (on settled cases) and the additional commissions I can expect if all my cases settle. If there is ever any question on whether I received payment on a case, I have the record in my Commissions Paid Record showing how each check was applied. By keeping a running total in this record, I also know how much I earned per year.

I also have found the Sales Record useful in other ways. When I am called upon to list a house by a client whom I represented many years before, I can go back to the entry in my Sales Record and immediately know the type of sale (VA, FHA, etc.), the selling price and date of sale. I can look this up while we are talking on the phone. It makes a good impression, when I am able to "remember" the price that my client's house sold for several years ago.

Having Fun and Making Money Too

Many people are curious about all phases of real estate selling. Perhaps they have just read a book on "How to Make a Million in Real Estate." *Money* is the magic magnet. Everybody wants some of it. Real estate is something everyone knows about. When a homeowner calls a real estate company for help in selling his home, he knows that he will have to pay a commission. He generally feels that it is a lot of money for little effort. When I am called in to list a house and walk in all smiles and good cheer, they are thinking: "She is making all that money and having fun too!" Sometimes a client tells me that he has been planning to become a real estate salesman because he has a free evening each week and wants to make a lot of money. He then asks my advice about which real estate company he should consider. I always listen seriously. (You need a sense of humor!) Of course, I tell the client that it isn't as easy as it looks and that not everyone makes a lot of money, but I'm sure he doesn't believe this. Then I just continue trying to get that listing (or make the sale) while chatting in a friendly manner. Real estate is a highly competitive field. The successful agents put a lot of time and effort into their work. Successful agents invest their money wisely, so that it can then *work for them*. Real estate is fun and exciting, and more so when you are making money, too.

Now That You're Earning It, What Do You Do With It?

As my commission checks started coming in, I realized I had a problem. My husband was already making a good salary and now half of what I earned would be siphoned for income taxes. I had worked too hard earning those commission checks and hated to part with that much of each one. I quickly found out how real estate investments can shelter income from taxes and have been using this kind of investment ever since, not only for myself, but for my clients as well. My husband and I started investing my earnings in houses as soon as I could accumulate enough cash for each down payment. As prices of houses continued to spiral up, so did the equities on the homes we had bought.

As a smart and successful real estate salesman, you should make your earnings work for you. However, also keep adequate funds in a savings account (where it draws only limited interest). That will be the fund that you can draw on in a hurrry, in case of an emergency (liquid investment). Other capital should be placed in long-term growth type investments, as real estate, with the advantages already mentioned. Since you, the real estate salesman, are already familiar with the real estate market, you should seriously consider this type of investment especially if your family income is high. You might also consider buying second mortgages at a discount, as such opportunities will often arise in the real estate business. Be aware of the risks involved and seek advice from an experienced associate if your experience is limited. Watch the housing market closely for the right time and conditions.

When investing in houses, try to work as much as possible with the bank's money. Look for a house that can be purchased with the least amount of money down, and one that is sure to appreciate in value in the future. You know that the more real estate you purchase, the more tax depreciation expense you can claim, and the less income tax you will have to pay during your most active selling years. Later, when you are ready to retire, you can either live on the rental income derived from these houses, or sell them individually when you have gone into a lower income tax bracket (because of retirement) and therefore pay less in capital gains taxes.

Most real estate offices will lower the commission charges for sales made to their own agents. In any case, if you do not have this option, you are still entitled to your commission as the selling agent. Read about and become familiar with investments and learn to actually use *appreciation, leverage, depreciation, tax shelters, estate building,* etc. Put yourself in the place of the investor, instead of the salesman, and reread the section on "Investors as Clients" in Chapter Three of this book.

Perhaps you do not wish to be bothered with managing rental houses, or perhaps the properties in your own area are not suitable for rental investments. You can still invest in real estate with its various advantages—through participation in triple net leases, limited partnerships that own apartment buildings or office buildings and similar enterprises. Many of these not only have the advantages of depreciation expenses, high leverage, appreciation and good yields, but also an added first year's accounting loss, which may be 75% to 100% of your investment. (This is usually for sales commissions, advance interest, etc., called the "front end" or "soft" expenses.) There are specialists who sell such investments and you should be able to locate them.

Now That You've Earned It, Don't Forget to Enjoy It!

In my first year as a real estate agent, I was so absorbed in the work I was doing, that I kept putting off taking a vacation. However, once I started to take them, I found that there is nothing like it to feel rejuvenated and raring to go when you return. You can regard your work as drudgery, with its wild hours and unscheduled mealtimes, or you can enjoy it with the knowledge of the benefits that your commissions will provide. There are surely many other ways to keep active, but I can't think of a single, more enjoyable way that involves so much challenge and excitement and monetary rewards too.

GLOSSARY

ABSTRACT OF TITLE ▪ A chronological condensed summary of all recorded instruments and history of ownership affecting title to a particular property.

ACCELERATION CLAUSE ▪ A clause generally found in a deed of trust, mortgage or note, that stipulates that in the event of a default of any of its covenants during the term of the loan, the entire debt is immediately due and must be paid in full.

ACCESS RIGHTS ▪ The right that an owner of a property has to passage over adjoining land, in order to enter and leave his property.

ACKNOWLEDGMENT ▪ A formal certification of a signature on a document made before an authorized officer (e.g., notary public) by a person who states that such was his act and deed.

AFFIDAVIT ▪ A voluntary written statement, sworn to or affirmed before an officer who has authority to administer such oath.

AGENCY ▪ An agreement, express or implied, between an agent and his principal, wherein the agent acts as his representative in dealing with a third party.

AGREEMENT OF SALE ▪ A written contract whereby a seller agrees to sell and a buyer agrees to buy under specific terms and conditions set forth therein.

AIR RIGHTS ▪ The rights to the use of the open space above a property owned or leased by the holder of the real estate.

AMORTIZATION TABLE ▪ A printed schedule listing the required monthly payments necessary in order to repay a loan with specified interest rate, if any, and for a definite time period.

ANNUITY ▪ An investment yielding fixed payments during the holder's life or for a stated number of years.

APPRAISAL ▪ An estimate or opinion of value set forth by one qualified to make such an opinion.

APPRAISAL BY CAPITALIZATION ▪ An estimate based on the net return that a property will bring.

APPRAISAL BY COMPARISON ▪ Estimating the value of a property by comparing it with other similar properties of known value.

APPRAISAL BY SUMMATION ▪ Estimating the value of a property by adding together factors that have been appraised separately, in order to form the whole (e.g., the cost of reproduction of a building plus the value of the land, less the depreciation).

AS IS ▪ These two words, inserted in a contract of sale, mean that no guarantees are given regarding the subject property. It is being purchased as it is.

ASSESSED VALUE ▪ A value assigned to a property by an assessor or government board for taxation and other purposes.

ASSESSMENT ▪ A non-recurring charge levied against real estate in the form of a tax, to cover the proportionate cost of an improvement, such as street or sewer.

ASSIGNMENT ▪ Transfer in writing, of title or interest in some instrument, such as a contract, from one person to another.

ASSUMPTION OF MORTGAGE ▪ Becoming personally liable for the payment and terms of a mortgage usually when taking title to the property mortgaged.

BALLOON PAYMENT ▪ The final amount due on a note where the periodic monthly payments do not completely amortize the loan at the time of its termination.

BEDROOM COMMUNITY ▪ An expression used for a complex of homes in a suburban area that is self-contained but has no major local sources for employment, and where the wage earners are gone during the day to a metropolitan area.

BINDER ▪ A preliminary written agreement to cover a down payment on the part of the purchaser. It is temporary in nature until a more formal contract can be drawn.

BIRD DOG ▪ An expression that refers to a salesman who "flushes out" prospects or listings which he turns over to a more experienced agent or to his broker.

BLANKET MORTGAGE ▪ A single mortgage covering two or more pieces of property.

BLOCK BUSTING ▪ An unethical real estate practice of moving one or more families of another race or creed into a neighborhood and then exploiting the situation by creating fear and unrest among the residents and urging them to sell their homes at deflated prices.

BOND ▪ A written instrument, secured by a mortgage or deed of trust on real estate, guaranteeing the repayment of a loan to the bearer at a designated time in the future.

BOOK VALUE ▪ The cost of a property plus additions and improvements, less the accrued depreciation.

BOOT ▪ A term used where property is being traded and the exchange is not exactly equal. The cash or other properties and services which are included to compensate for any difference in value is called the boot.

BRIDGE LOAN ▪ A short term loan, usually made by a real estate company or a financial institution to a homeowner who is selling his home and purchasing another, but must settle on the new one first. This loan is generally repaid on settlement of the homeowner's own home. Also called "Interim Loan."

BUILDING CODE ▪ A standard of rules and regulations set up to regulate the construction of buildings, usually by a government body.

BUILDING LINE ▪ An established line at a specified distance from the front of a lot within which a building must be constructed.

BUILDING PERMIT ▪ A permit which grants the right to start construction work or make alterations on a property according to the plans and specifications submitted with an application.

BUILDING RESTRICTIONS ▪ Zoning, regulatory requirements or clauses within a deed, which limit the type or size of a building and which is recorded to protect usage by future property owners.

BUILT-INS ▪ Stationary equipment, such as appliances or bookcases, permanently affixed to a house, which become real property by nature of their installation.

BUY-BACK AGREEMENT ▪ An agreement in which a seller has the option to repurchase his property within a given time and for a specified price.

BUYER'S MARKET ▪ When the supply of a particular type of property is much greater than the demand.

CALL-IN ▪ A phone inquiry concerning the listing or selling of property, made to a real estate office.

CANCELLATION CLAUSE ▪ A clause written into some contracts and leases, giving one or both parties the right to cancel the contract under specified circumstances.

CAPITAL GAIN ▪ Profit from the sale of a capital asset. If the asset has been held for more than the number of months specified in the current tax law (e.g. 12 months after December 31, 1977) it is considered long-term and qualifies for special tax treatment.

CARRY OVER CLAUSE ▪ This clause is found in exclusive listing agreements and protects the broker for a specified time beyond the date of expiration. Should a property so listed be sold after the listing has expired, to one to whom it was shown while still in effect, the broker will be considered the procuring cause of the transaction.

CEILING RATE ▪ The maximum amount as established that can be charged as rent or fee.

CERTIFICATE OF ELIGIBILITY ▪ A certificate issued by the government which verifies an individual's entitlement to the benefits of the Servicemen's Readjustment Act of 1944.

CERTIFICATE OF OCCUPANCY ▪ A permit issued by a building department verifying that work on the building complies with local zoning ordinances and that people may occupy the building.

CERTIFICATE OF REASONABLE VALUE (C.R.V.) ▪ A appraisal commitment issued by the Veteran's Administration that sets the value on a property to be purchased by a veteran under the G.I. Bill.

CERTIFICATE OF RECORDATION ▪ A certificate verifying that an instrument has been duly recorded by the County Recorder's office.

CERTIFICATE OF RELEASE ▪ A document signed by a lender, stating that a mortgage has been paid and its indebtedness fully satisfied.

CERTIFICATE OF TITLE ▪ A certificate issued by a title company, based on an examination of record titles, as to the condition of title for a particular real estate property. This carries no guarantee nor does it offer protection to the purchaser against hidden defects in the title.

CLEAR TITLE ▪ Good, marketable title; one that is free of encumbrances.

CLIENT ▪ In real estate, the person who employs the agent and is responsible for the payment of the commission or fee. The principal.

CLOSING COSTS ▪ The various expenses both buyer and seller incur in the transfer of ownership of real property.

CLOSING STATEMENT ▪ A detailed final accounting of all debits and credits for the buyer and seller, which summarizes the costs involved in the sale of property.

CLOUD ON TITLE ▪ Any outstanding claim or encumbrance affecting title transfer which prevents the buyer from receiving a clear title.

CODE OF ETHICS ▪ The accepted standard of professional conduct and behavior in transacting real estate. It sets forth the rules and principles governing the relationship of members of the National Association of Real Estate Boards. Basically, the underlying theme is embodied in the golden rule: "Do unto others as you would have them do unto you."

COLD CANVAS ▪ A method of obtaining listings by going from door to door, asking each owner if he is thinking of selling his home or if he knows anyone who plans to sell.

COMMITMENT ▪ A pledge or promise to perform. In real estate, a written commitment is generally given by a lending institution, which states the specific terms of the mortgage loan it will give in the event of a sale.

COMMON PROPERTY ▪ Property that is owned and used by people who live in an area and is open to the equal use by all who own it or have a public interest in it.

COMMUNITY PROPERTY ▪ Property owned jointly by husband and wife and accumulated through the joint efforts of both living together as husband and wife. (Property owned before, or after termination of a marriage or acquired through inheritance, is individually owned.)

CO-MORTGAGOR ▪ A signer of a mortgage or deed of trust, who assumes equal responsibility for its repayment.

COMPARABLES ▪ Properties similar to the one being priced, on which asking prices and/or selling prices are known.

COMPLETION BOND ▪ A performance bond that is posted by a contractor in which he guarantees that he will satisfactorily complete a project and that it will be free of liens. The bonding company makes good if the contractor fails to perform.

CONDEMNATION ▪ The taking of private property for public use by the right of eminent domain. A government's right to declare a structure unsafe or unfit for human habitation. Its use is prevented until specified defects have been remedied.

CONDITIONAL SALES CONTRACT ▪ A contract to sell whereby possession is given to the buyer, but title remains with the seller until certain required acts are accomplished, such as full payment of the consideration.

CONDOMINIUM ▪ Individual ownership of a single unit in a multiple unit building, where the owner has a deed in fee title to the space he owns and is permitted to sell, mortgage or bequeath his ownership rights in the same manner as he would if he owned a single family house. Certain common areas, however, are owned jointly with the other owners.

CONSIDERATION ▪ Anything of value (usually money) given to influence and induce a person to enter into a contract. It can consist of personal services or just "love and affection."

CONSTRUCTION LOAN ▪ A loan given to a builder which generally provides for periodic payments to the builder as each phase of construction is completed.

CONTINGENCY ▪ Any requirement which is a part of a contract and which must be satisfied before the contract can be considered ready for performance.

CONTINGENT LISTING ▪ A listing on a property which is dependent on the sale or purchase of another property, or on any other specified condition.

CONTRACT ▪ A binding agreement entered into by two or more competent parties who exchange mutual promises concerning performance, in accordance with their mutual wishes.

CONVENTIONAL LOAN ▪ In real estate, this type of mortgage loan is generally granted by a bank or savings and loan association, has real estate as the security and is not guaranteed by a government agency.

COOPERATING BROKERS ▪ Two or more brokers working together to bring about a successful real estate transaction. The commissions are generally shared on a 50/50 basis.

COOPERATIVE OWNERSHIP (CO-OP) ▪ In this type of ownership, the tenants of the building become stockholders in a corporation, each receiving stock equal to his investment, which corporation owns the building. This differs from condominium ownership, where fee title is actually passed to individual owners of each unit.

COUNTEROFFER ▪ A new offer as to price, terms or conditions, which is made in reply to a prior unacceptable one and which terminates the original offer.

CREAM PUFF ▪ In real estate, a house or other real estate that is in prime condition, shows well, and should be easy to sell.

CREDIT REPORT ▪ A report covering the credit history of a person or business.

CUL-DE-SAC ▪ A dead end street with a circular turning area, for convenient entrance and exit.

CURTSY RIGHT ▪ In some states, the right which a husband has in his wife's estate at her death.

DEED ▪ A written instrument under seal, which when signed by the grantor and delivered, transfers title to real property.

DEED OF TRUST ▪ In some areas of the country, a deed of trust is used in place of a mortgage. The deed is placed in trust with a third party to insure payment of an indebtedness or to assure that other conditions of the transaction are met. After all the conditions have been satisfied, the third party then delivers the deed to the purchaser, thereby freeing him from any further responsibility.

DEPARTMENT OF HOUSING AND URBAN DEVELOPMENT (HUD) ▪ Government agency established in 1965 to coordinate and expand housing programs.

DEPRECIATION ▪ The gradual decline of value in property caused by deterioration, obsolescence or various other factors.

DEVELOPED LAND ▪ Land that has been improved by adding roads and bringing in utilities, landscaping or the construction of buildings.

DEVELOPMENT ▪ A subdivision that has homes, shopping centers, recreation areas, parks, schools and churches.

DISBURSEMENTS ▪ In real estate, the money expended by buyer and seller in order to transfer ownership. (See Closing Costs.)

DISPOSSESS ▪ To take legal action to deprive one of possession or occupancy of a real estate property.

DISTRESSED PROPERTY ▪ Property located in a blighted area or where the market value is diminishing and which has to be sold at a lower price.

DOCUMENTARY STAMPS ▪ A tax in the form of stamps, attached to deeds and mortgages, when a real estate title passes from one owner to another.

DOWER ▪ The legal right which a wife has in her husband's estate at his death, but not applicable in states with community property laws.

DRY ROT ▪ A major cause of deterioration in older buildings. It is a fungus growth on wood or other materials caused by water leakage.

EARNEST MONEY ▪ A purchaser's down payment for real estate, as evidence of good faith.

EASEMENT ▪ The right or privilege of an individual to another person's land or property (e.g., a right of way).

ENCUMBRANCE ▪ Any legal right or claim binding upon real property that burdens the title and diminishes its value (e.g., liens, mortgages, easements or pending legal action).

ENTITLEMENT ▪ A legal right under the G.I. Bill, whereby the veteran is eligible for a government guaranteed loan. (*See* Certificate of Eligibility.)

EQUITY ▪ The interest in or value which an owner has in real property over and above all existing indebtednesses.

ESCALATOR CLAUSE ▪ A provision in many leases, providing for increased payments in the event of specific occurrences such as increase in taxes, insurance and other items, to be passed on to the tenant.

ESCAPE CLAUSE ▪ A clause in an agreement, which permits one or more of the parties to withdraw from the agreement or to modify it.

ESCROW ▪ Something of value such as money, deed, bond or real property, which is given to a third party for delivery upon the fulfillment or performance of some act or condition, at which time the escrow may be released.

EXAMINATION OF TITLE ▪ A search of the records to determine the status of the title to a property in order to ascertain if there are any liens, easements, encumbrances or clouds on the title.

EXCLUSIVE AGENCY ▪ A written instrument designating one real estate broker as sole agent for the sale of a property for a designated period of time, but which permits the owner to rent or sell by himself without paying a commission.

EXCLUSIVE RIGHT TO SELL ▪ An exclusive listing designating a broker to sell, lease or negotiate a property for a specified period of time to the exclusion of all others, in which the broker is entitled to a commission in the event of sale by another broker, or by the owner himself.

FEDERAL HOUSING ADMINISTRATION (FHA) ▪ Founded in 1934, it was established by the National Housing Act to provide mortgage insurance to approved lending institutions for financing homes and apartments. It does not, however, furnish the funds.

FEDERAL NATIONAL MORTGAGE ASSOCIATION (FNMA) ▪ The secondary mortgage market operated by the Federal Government for federally insured loans. Also called "Fannie Mae."

Fee Simple ■ Ownership in real property where the owner has absolute good and marketable title to the property conveyed to him.

FHA Loan ■ A mortgage loan insured by the Federal Housing Administration and offered to purchasers who qualify under FHA requirements.

Finder's Fee ■ As applied to real estate, a fee paid to another for furnishing a buyer or property listing, or for information which is beneficial to an agent in arranging a sale.

First Mortgage ■ The mortgage on a property that is superior to and takes precedence over all other mortgages.

First Refusal ■ A person's right to have first privilege to buy or lease real estate, or meet any offer made by another.

Floor Time ■ Time allowed an agent to handle all incoming phone calls and walk-ins at the real estate office, and to get the benefit of the leads which result.

Foreclosure ■ A legal action instituted by a mortgagee for sale of a property which has been pledged against payment of a debt.

Forfeiture ■ Loss of anything of value or money, because of failure to perform under the terms of an agreement.

Franchise ■ A special right or privilege granted to an individual or company.

Franchised Broker ■ A local broker who is part of a national chain, which does joint advertising and uses a trade name.

Free and Clear ■ Free of all indebtedness. Property without a current mortgage or one which has been paid in full.

Front Foot Value ■ The value of a property expressed in terms of its footage on a main street or watercourse. Land so measured is understood to extend the depth of the lot.

Gift Letter ■ A letter which verifies that certain sums of money are a gift from a relative and made without obligation for repayment, and are to be used for acquiring real property.

G.I. Loan ■ A Veteran's Administration guaranteed loan available to qualified veterans. This loan can be used for buying, building, repairing and improving real property.

GOVERNMENT NATIONAL MORTGAGE ASSOCIATION (GNMA) ■ A federal agency under HUD which sells bonds to raise funds for direct mortgage loans and handles direct subsidies for housing projects approved by Congress. Also called "Ginnie Mae."

GRACE PERIOD ■ A period of time provided for by most mortgages, covering the time when a mortgage payment or other debt becomes due and before it goes into default, during which time it can be paid without penalty or default.

GRADUATED LEASE ■ A lease providing for a stated rent for a fixed period of time, followed by an increase or decrease in rent at later periods.

GRANT DEED ■ Used in certain states, it is an instrument used to convey title to real property and carries implied warranties.

GROSS LEASE ■ A lease for real property whereby the owner-lessor pays all the normal property charges incurred through ownership.

GROUND RENT ■ Rent paid for the possession and use of land rather than for the building upon it, or that amount of the rent which should be properly credited to the land.

GUARANTEED LOAN ■ A loan in which the lender is guaranteed payment or partial payment in the event of default (e.g., Veteran's Administration loans are guaranteed by the government up to a specified amount).

HIGH RISE ■ Generally used to describe an apartment house higher than three floors.

HOMEOWNER'S POLICY ■ An insurance policy "package" on a house which covers numerous items not insured under a standard fire policy.

HYPOTHECATE ■ A pledge of property as security for a debt without the necessity of actually giving up its possession.

IMPERFECT TITLE ■ A title that does not pass on the complete fee and is defective and therefore not marketable or insurable.

IMPROVED LAND ■ Additions made to and on real property that enhance its value, such as grading, roads, sidewalks and structures of all kinds.

INCOME PROPERTY ▪ Property that may be commercial, residential or industrial, and purchased primarily for the monetary return it will net (e.g., commercial and residential rents).

INSTALLMENT SALES CONTRACT ▪ Purchase of real estate whereby the buyer receives possession of the property by making deferred payments at regular intervals. He does not, however, receive title to it until the purchase price is reached. Should he default, payments already made are forfeited.

INSTITUTE OF REAL ESTATE BROKERS (I.R.E.B.) ▪ A division of the National Association of Real Estate Boards. Many real estate brokers and their sales agents subscribe to this service which furnishes current real estate material to its members.

INSTITUTIONAL LENDER ▪ Any bank, mortgage company or insurance company authorized to invest depositors' funds in mortgages, as opposed to private lenders who invest their own money.

INSTRUMENT ▪ A written legal document used in transacting legal business (e.g., deed, contract, lease, mortgage, etc.).

INSURED LOAN ▪ A loan where the lender is guaranteed full or partial payment should the borrower default.

INTERIM FINANCING ▪ Temporary, short term loan, generally in effect during the construction of a building.

JOINT TENANCY ▪ Ownership of property by two or more persons with equal and undivided ownership, plus the right of survivorship.

JUDGMENT LIEN ▪ An encumbrance that binds the land of a debtor so that its proceeds can be used to pay a debt.

KEY LOT ▪ A lot that is strategically located adjacent to a corner lot's rear property line, but fronting on another street. This type of lot has added market value.

KICK-OUT CLAUSE ▪ In a contingency contract, a clause which permits a secondary contract offer to be written and if accepted, the original purchaser under the primary contract has a specified time to remove his contingency or his primary contract becomes void.

LANDLOCKED ▪ A parcel of land which has no public road frontage and requires an easement over adjoining property in order to be reached.

LEASE ▪ A contract between the owner of a property (lessor) and a tenant (lessee) for rental at a stipulated time, and setting forth the terms and conditions upon which the tenant may occupy and use the property.

LEASEBACK AGREEMENT ▪ An agreement containing a provision which is a condition of the sale, whereby the seller leases the property after the sale, from the buyer.

LESSEE ▪ The one to whom a property is being leased. The tenant.

LESSOR ▪ The one who holds title to a property being leased. The landlord.

LEVERAGE ▪ Effective use of money, usually accomplished by investing the least amount of capital possible and using borrowed funds, in order to bring a maximum percentage of return.

LIEN ▪ A claim or encumbrance upon a property whereby the property serves as the security (e.g., mortgages, trust deeds, taxes, judgments, etc.).

LIMITED PARTNERSHIP ▪ A partnership arrangement in which each party has liability limited to the amount he has invested. A limited partner is an investor and has no voice in management.

LIQUID ASSETS ▪ Any property that can be readily converted to cash.

LIQUIDATED DAMAGES ▪ A sum agreed upon to be paid in the event of breach of contract.

LISTING ▪ A contract employing a real estate broker and authorizing the payment of a fee for the performance of services in connection with specified real estate.

LOCK BOX ▪ A metal container which holds a key to the house being offered for sale. It is secured on the door or knob and permits all real estate agents with a master key to gain entry for showing purposes.

M.A.I. ▪ Abbreviation for Member of Appraiser's Institute; a group of extremely qualified appraisers who have passed the rigid standards set by the Institute.

MARKETABLE TITLE ▪ A title free from any encumbrances or clouds which is transferrable.

MARKET PRICE ▪ The price a property brings when widely offered for sale.

MECHANIC'S LIEN ▪ A lien which exists in favor of an individual who has furnished materials or labor for the construction, improvement or repair of a building, but who has not been paid.

MONTH TENANCY ▪ A lease which permits a tenant to remain in the premises from one month to another, continuing to pay rent after the original termination date is passed.

MORTGAGE ▪ A pledge of property given as security for payment of a debt or the fulfillment of an obligation.

MORTGAGE BANKERS ▪ Firms that use their own capital for mortgage loans, later selling them to permanent investors.

MORTGAGE BROKER ▪ An individual or company that locates lending institutions, insurance companies and private sources that will lend money for mortgages, but does not use his own capital to do so.

MORTGAGEE ▪ A person who lends money and to whom a mortgage is given to secure the loan.

MORTGAGE INSURANCE ▪ A policy written to cover the amount of a mortgage on property, whereby the balance of the loan is paid in full upon the death of the mortgagor.

MORTGAGOR ▪ The owner of a property who borrows the money being secured by a mortgage.

MULTIPLE LISTING SERVICE (MLS) ▪ A cooperative method of listing and selling property that is offered by some Boards of Realtors, whereby each subscribing broker brings his listings to the attention of other members for wider market exposure.

N.A.R.E.B. ▪ An abbreviation for the National Association of Real Estate Boards.

NET LEASE ▪ A lease where the tenant pays all costs of maintenance and the landlord gets rent which is a fixed amount, but the landlord is responsible for taxes and insurance.

NET LISTING ▪ A listing wherein the agent retains as his commission all sums over and above a net price previously agreed upon with the owner.

NET-NET-NET LEASE ▪ Also called a "Triple-Net" Lease. A lease where the tenant pays all costs of maintenance, all taxes and insurance. The landlord gets a fixed amount as rent, no matter what these items cost.

NOTE ▪ A written, signed instrument, attesting to a debt.

NULL AND VOID ▪ Cancelled and invalid. Having no legal force and therefore not binding.

OCCUPANCY AGREEMENT ▪ An agreement made where the purchaser is permitted to occupy the premises prior to settlement under certain terms and conditions. Also called Pre-Occupancy Agreement.

OPEN END MORTGAGE ▪ A mortgage which permits the mortgagor to increase the loan amount without additional loan placement charges, and at the same interest rate.

OPEN HOUSE ▪ A house that is for sale, which is advertised and held open to the public for inspection during specified hours on the advertised day.

OPEN LISTING ▪ A non-exclusive listing, given to one or more brokers, with the selling commission going to whichever broker procures the buyer. The seller, moreover, reserves the right to sell the property himself without payment of commission.

OPTION ▪ The right given, for a consideration, to purchase or lease a property at a specified price during a designated period.

ORIGINATION FEE ▪ Points charged by a lender.

O.S.P. ▪ Abbreviation for "off street parking" as used on most listing forms.

O.W.T. ▪ Abbreviation for "owner will take." On listing forms, this refers to the willingness of a seller of property to take back a second trust.

OVER-IMPROVEMENT ▪ An improvement to property which is not the highest and best use for the site on which it is placed, by reason of its excessive cost or extensive size, and where it becomes almost impossible to regain the cost of such improvements when sold.

PERCOLATION TEST ▪ Sometimes called the "Perk Test." A soil test to determine whether the ground will absorb sufficient water for the installation of a septic tank.

PERSONAL PROPERTY ▪ All articles of property other than real estate, which are not permanently affixed to the land or building.

PEST CONTROL CLAUSE ▪ A clause written into most contracts of sale requiring the seller to guarantee the property against termite infestation or to correct the condition should it be found to exist.

PITI ▪ Abbreviation for "Principal, Interest, Taxes and Insurance" which are the normal monthly carrying charges of a mortgage on a residence.

PLAT ▪ A map or plan showing the lots and blocks of a subdivision, or an individual parcel of land and its dimensions.

POCKET LISTING ▪ A listing that a real estate salesman "pockets" and keeps hidden from his associates to his own benefit. This is not considered an ethical practice.

POINTS ▪ A term used by lenders when making additional charges, where one point represents one percent of the mortgage amount being loaned. Also called an "Origination Fee."

POST-OCCUPANCY AGREEMENT ▪ An agreement in which the seller is permitted to remain on the premises as a tenant under specified terms and conditions, after the house has been sold and settled.

POWER OF ATTORNEY ▪ A written authority where one person can represent another as his "attorney-in-fact" to carry out specific acts.

PREPAYMENT PENALTY ▪ A charge imposed on a mortgagor for paying the mortgage balance before it is due.

PROMISSORY NOTE ▪ Written evidence of indebtedness and promise to pay by a specified date.

PROPERTY TAX ▪ A tax levied on real or personal property.

PUBLIC HOUSING ADMINISTRATION ▪ The functions of this government agency have been assumed by the Department of Housing and Urban Development.

PURCHASE MONEY MORTGAGE ▪ Also called a "Trust Deed," this mortgage is given by a buyer to a seller in part payment of the purchase price of real estate.

PURCHASE OFFER ▪ An offer to buy. It is a unilateral contract until signed and accepted by the seller.

QUIT CLAIM DEED ▪ A deed of conveyance whereby the grantor relinquishes any claim in a property that would constitute a cloud upon the title.

REAL ESTATE BOARD ▪ A private real estate organization formed to improve the real estate profession and promote cooperation and ethical practices among real estate agents.

REAL ESTATE SETTLEMENT PROCEDURES ACT (R.E.S.P.A.) ▪ A 1975 Federal law requiring specific settlement disclosures and procedures by lenders, in order to protect home buyers.

REAL PROPERTY ▪ The rights, title and interest in land and the improvements thereon.

REALTOR ▪ An active member of a local real estate board, affiliated with the National Association of Real Estates Boards (incorporated for the advancement of the interests of real estate brokers and the protection of the public).

REFERRAL ▪ In real estate, a client or prospect who has been obtained through another's recommendation.

RENT CONTROL ▪ State or local laws that regulate and limit the amount of rent a landlord can charge.

REVENUE STAMPS ▪ Documentary stamps which are affixed to real estate documents showing payment of government tax.

RIGHT OF SURVIVORSHIP ▪ The right held by a surviving joint tenant to acquire the interest of the deceased tenant.

RIGHT OF WAY ▪ An easement over the property belonging to another.

ROOKIE ▪ A new real estate agent, generally during the first year.

SATISFACTION OF MORTGAGE ▪ An instrument that acknowledges payment in full of a mortgage or deed of trust, and is recorded.

SECONDARY CONTRACT OFFER ▪ A second offer taken on property for sale, which is contingent on the primary contract being negated.

SECONDARY MORTGAGE MARKET ▪ The process whereby lenders sell primary mortgages in bulk to investors, in order to make more funds available. (See "Fannie Mae".)

SECURITY DEPOSIT ▪ A deposit made by a prospective purchaser or tenant to guarantee payment of an obligation and performance of an agreement.

SELLER'S MARKET ▪ When the demand for a particular type of property is much greater than the supply.

SETTLEMENT ▪ In real estate, the transfer of title. A closing.

SPECIAL ASSESSMENTS ▪ A levy on property for a specific public improvement to it, or in the immediate area.

SPECIAL WARRANTY DEED ▪ A deed often used by trustees in the transfer of title, whereby the grantor limits his liability to the grantee.

SPOT ZONING ▪ Zoning in limited areas that differ from the zoning of the general area immediately surrounding it.

STANDARD TITLE POLICY ▪ The title policy which a buyer of real property sometimes receives, which insures against all defects of record, but excludes other items.

STRAIGHT LINE DEPRECIATION ▪ A method of calculating an allowance for depreciation of a structure by setting aside a fixed sum each year.

SUBJECT TO MORTGAGE ▪ Taking title to property with an existing mortgage, but assuming no personal liability towards payment of the debt unless so indicated.

SUBLEASE ▪ A lease given by a tenant to another, under the terms of an existing primary lease on the premises.

SUBORDINATION CLAUSE ▪ A clause in an instrument stating that a lien or a mortgage shall be inferior to subsequent liens or encumbrances.

SURVEY ▪ A map or plat showing the lines of possession and dimensions of a parcel of land.

TAX SHELTER ▪ Income property that permits the owner to deduct for depreciation and other expenses so that the taxable income is minimized, although there is cash income.

TENANCY BY THE ENTIRETY (T/E) ▪ A joint estate owned by husband and wife, with rights of survivorship, which cannot be terminated without mutual consent of both parties.

TENANCY IN COMMON ▪ Ownership in property by two or more individuals, each possessing a separate undivided interest, with no right of survivorship.

TERMITE CLAUSE ▪ A clause embodied in most contracts of sale, requiring that the house being sold must pass inspection and be certified as free from termite infestation.

"TIME IS OF THE ESSENCE" CLAUSE ▪ A clause in a contract that places great emphasis on completing the terms and conditions by the time specified in the contract, and that failure to do so will be considered a violation of the contract.

TITLE ▪ Evidence and proof of lawful ownership of property and right to its legal possession.

TITLE INSURANCE ▪ An insurance policy issued to the owner of a property and/or his mortgagee against defect in title for as long as he owns the property.

TRANSFER CLAUSE ▪ A clause in a lease which cancels the agreement should the tenant be required to move to another area because of job transfer.

TRUST FUND ▪ In real estate, a fund set up by a lender for the benefit of a mortgagor to meet the tax and insurance payments when due. An escrow account.

TRUTH-IN-LENDING ▪ Disclosure requirements required by law on the part of lenders.

UNILATERAL CONTRACT ▪ A contract in which only one party is bound by the terms of the agreement. An example is an offer to purchase signed by the purchaser only. It can be recalled or voided at any time prior to the second party's agreement.

UNIMPROVED LAND ▪ Land without buildings or other improvements.

VARIABLE RATE MORTGAGE (V.R.M.) ▪ A mortgage which permits the interest rate to change during its term and therefore the monthly payments for principal and interest may not be constant.

VARIANCE ▪ A special request for change in existing zoning laws for a property.

VETERAN'S ADMINISTRATION (VA) ▪ An agency of the federal government set up to administer the laws enacted for the benefit of veterans, their families and beneficiaries.

VETERAN'S EXEMPTION ▪ In some states, the veteran who is a property owner is allowed a tax exemption on a portion of his tax bill.

V.R.M. ▪ Abbreviation for "Variable Rate Mortgage."

WALK-IN ▪ A prospect who walks into the real estate office in order to list or buy a property, to rent, or to obtain information and advice.

WARRANTY DEED ▪ A written instrument used in most states that guarantees to the grantee and his heirs good title, and is the highest form of deed.

WRAP-AROUND MORTGAGE ▪ A refinancing technique whereby a seller of property continues payment of the existing mortgage which carries a low interest rate, and gives a new mortgage to the purchaser at a higher interest rate.

YIELD ▪ The annual dollar return on an investment or property, usually expressed as a percentage of the total investment.

ZONING ▪ The division of an area by the proper authorities into separate districts reserved for different uses, such as residential, business, heavy industry, etc.

INDEX